The Self Assessment Handbook

This book is dedicated to the leaders and employees of the European Foundation for Quality Management, the American National Institute of Standards and Technology, and the British Quality Foundation, who have had the vision and determination to create their Award and Measurement Processes.

The Self Assessment Handbook
For corporate excellence

Chris Hakes
with contributions from
Barry Popplewell, Hugh Gallacher and Gill Clements

BRISTOL
QUALITY
CENTRE

CHAPMAN & HALL
London · Glasgow · Weinheim · New York · Tokyo · Melbourne · Madras

Published by Chapman & Hall, 2–6 Boundary Row, London SE1 8HN, UK

Chapman & Hall, 2–6 Boundary Row, London SE1 8HN, UK

Blackie Academic & Professional, Wester Cleddens Road, Bishopbriggs, Glasgow G64 2NZ, UK

Chapman & Hall GmbH, Pappelallee 3, 69469 Weinheim, Germany

Chapman & Hall Inc., One Penn Plaza, 41st Floor, New York NY 10119, USA

Chapman & Hall Japan, Thomson Publishing Japan, Hirakawacho Nemoto Building, 6F, 1–7–11 Hirakawa-cho, Chiyoda-ku, Tokyo 102, Japan

Chapman & Hall Australia, Thomas Nelson Australia, 102 Dodds Street, South Melbourne, Victoria 3205, Australia

Chapman & Hall India, R. Seshadri, 32 Second Main Road, CIT East, Madras 600 035, India

First edition 1994

© 1994 Bristol Quality Centre

Typeset by the Bristol Quality Centre
Printed in Great Britain by TJ Press (Padstow) Ltd., Padstow, Cornwall

ISBN 0 412 58660 6

A catalogue record for this book is available from the British Library

Printed on permanent acid-free text paper, manufactured in accordance with ANSI/NISO Z39.48–1992 and ANSI/NISO Z39.48–1984 (Permanence of Paper).

Contents

Acknowledgements

The authors involved in this publication wish to acknowledge and thank all those who have assisted, influenced or just helped to maintain sanity during the production of this book.

Particular thanks are due to our friends and colleagues at key award administrators such as the European Foundation for Quality Management, the USA's National Institute of Standards and Technology, and the British Quality Foundation.

Finally, thanks are due to those who have assisted us edit, type and produce this document. Your calm and patient assistance was invaluable.

1 Introduction

Achieving 'world class' status for your organization requires you to take a close look at your entire operation, your processes and your customers, and to compare yourself with the best. But starting this process can be a daunting prospect.

This book describes one of the fastest growing methods used by organizations to measure and achieve a World Class rating. That is the creative, regular and systematic self-application of the measures inherent within internationally acknowledged award processes used to recognize corporate excellence.

So what should you measure?...Ask any European-based expert to assess the well-being of an organization and the chances are that the response will still be based exclusively on the annual accounts. The gamut of financial data - profitability, assets, ratios and the like - will probably constitute the sole gauge of how that organization is doing.

But just how accurate a picture of an organization's condition can a purely finance-based analysis give? And perhaps more to the point, can it alone really give a meaningful indication of how that company might fare in the future?

The commonly held notion that corporate health and wealth are automatically one and the same leads many organizations to neglect key aspects of their operations. They do so at their peril, for important though financial indicators are, they can mislead. In any case, they are not necessarily relevant to the organization's capacity to adjust to current - and more importantly, future - market conditions.

Financial measures alone are clearly not the solution. Indeed, it can be argued that it matters little how well an organization has performed in the past - and that is all the annual accounts will tell you. What does count is whether or not it is equipped to adjust to the rapidly changing demands of today's marketplace.

With these thoughts in mind many organizations have been searching for alternatives among the measurement systems that exist worldwide. Most have concluded that, although many world class, best practice models have been developed throughout the years, the most credible, challenging and accepted are those that are contained within international award schemes such as the European and UK Quality Awards and the USA's Malcolm Baldrige National Quality Award (see Chapter 5).

This book focuses on the European and UK Quality Award process, this being commonly perceived as the best and most applied process for self assessment of European organizations. Details of other key internationally recognized schemes are provided where such information may add value.

By providing a 'Starter Kit' (Chapter 6) it aims to get newcomers to these processes quickly achieving benefits, whilst more seasoned users will value the analysis provided in the previous chapters.

This book is, in particular, about creative use of these measures through regular and systematic self assessment. It aims to help European organizations to achieve improvements in competitiveness and effectiveness. Those wishing to apply to win awards will also find it useful!

2 What are the benefits of self assessing corporate excellence?

If European organizations are to survive through the next decade, they must attract customers and triumph against the swelling ranks of highly sophisticated international competitors who now have easy access to European markets. Survival these days depends on a list of crucial factors including flexibility, efficiency, effectiveness...and a host of other virtues that can be grouped under the banner of 'corporate excellence'.

The successful organization must have dynamic, world class management practices and appropriate leadership - and that means using and honing its internal systems to effect an unrelenting improvement in the efficiency of the organization as a whole; it means using a comprehensive portfolio of measures, rather than focusing solely on finance which can encourage managers to act only for the short-term.

Executive managers now recognize these issues. They know that they must steer their organizations towards world class performance by identifying their current position, reacting to the ever-changing market and operational climates and by constantly reviewing the courses they sail.

More and more, they are using the models and frameworks established by either the Malcolm Baldrige National Quality Award or the European Quality Award as the means of assessing corporate excellence. Such models help managers to ascertain their current position and predict future behaviour, thus forming a basis for setting and reviewing plans and progress. It is from such measurements that many of the 'benefits' of self assessment arise.

These can be summarized as follows:

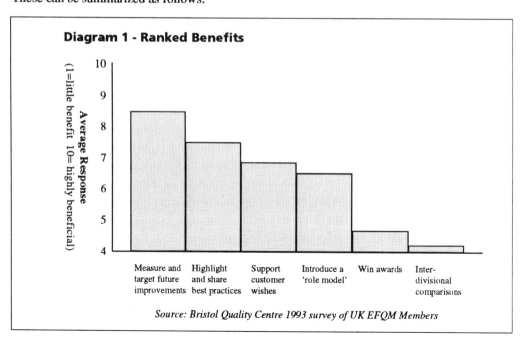

Diagram 1 - Ranked Benefits

Source: Bristol Quality Centre 1993 survey of UK EFQM Members

2.1 Benefit 1: Self assessment to measure and target improvements

A self assessment provides a strong predictor of long term survival. It does this through the objective identification of current strengths and areas for improvement by comparison with an accepted set of world class corporate excellence measures.

The results of such an assessment can be used by organizations to prioritize, target and measure progress towards excellence. At the same time, they provide an opportunity to ensure that activities designed to improve the operation are fully integrated with the organization's strategies and plans, and that any new initiatives are evaluated and measured against the framework. They are beginning to turn the 'religion' of total quality into a 'science'.

> *If you know your enemy and know yourself, you need not fear the result of a hundred battles.*
> *- attributed to Sun Tsu, a Chinese general 500BC*

The achievement of world class performance may be driven by visionary leadership or initiated through crisis-driven strategies (ref. 1 and 2). In both cases, self assessment helps measure the success and deployment of specific initiatives. For some, self assessment may equate to 'self-shocked' and provide an impetus for change through the realization of the potential long term effects of a lowly scoring organization.

2.2 Benefit 2: Self assessment to highlight and share best practices

By making comparisons against internal divisions, departments and externally against other organizations you can discover overlooked strengths and identify best practices.

The results of self assessment, based on the processes established by the major international awards, provide a growing common language through which organizations can 'benchmark'. Comparisons of either overall performance or through criteria are becoming common (see Chapter 5 for explanation of 'criteria').

Internally, several organizations have systematized this with internal recognition processes. For instance, AT&T have introduced a 'Chairman's Award' which has been credited with boosting the success of AT&T's Network Systems Group and their Universal Card Services, which have both won the Malcolm Baldrige National Quality Award, in the USA, in the same year.

Externally, a growing number of partnerships and networks exists to measure progress against award frameworks (see Appendix 2). Most of the award administrations publish data that enables organizations to compare their performance against overall norms. In this way general comparisons can be made, and the sharing of more specific information between organizations allows those organizations to compare themselves on a one-to-one basis.

2.3 Benefit 3: Self assessment to support customer objectives or requests

Assessment provides a useful analysis of an organization's capability and this is obviously of real interest to potential customers. These analyses give a far better picture of the potential suppliers than can be gained through normal supplier assessment approaches.

While the value of pursuing this in a systematic way continues to be debated, major purchasers increasingly expect their key suppliers to have self assessment processes. In the USA, award scheme assessment is said to have led to certain purchasers actively 'encouraging' suppliers to submit an application to the award organizations so that the feedback report they then receive can be cited during negotiations.

2.4 Benefit 4: Self assessment to provide strategic direction (to produce a visionary 'role model' of excellence)

Many organizations are now presenting a vision of their future with statements such as "We will be in a position to apply and win, should we choose, by the year 'xyz'". They then use the related self assessment processes to measure progress and integrate current and past initiatives such as customer focus, process re-engineering, TQM, and the like. Some users, perhaps slightly flippantly, have commented that this approach by providing overall direction, helps to overcome an organization's tendency to 'flip from one initiative, or flavour of the month, to the next'.

"Quality is an endless journey: like walking towards the horizon - no matter how far you walk, it does not change where the horizon is"
- Bernard Fournier, Managing Director of Rank Xerox, 1992 European Quality Award Winner.

It is worth noting that discussion of the self assessment results by an executive team will help to identify the current levels of 'commitment' felt by each member. This will highlight the corresponding degree of consensus in respect of the different elements of the frameworks used. This can be beneficial in promoting a feeling of involvement in, and ownership of, subsequent visions and plans. In this way, it can provide an opportunity for the company to build a greater unity, with common direction and an increased consistency of purpose in pursuit of initiatives to effect improvements. It can thus help to accelerate change.

2.5 Benefit 5: Applying to win awards?

Winning an award will obviously enhance the image and reputation of an organization. It is, however, notable that this potential benefit was ranked second to last in a recent Bristol Quality Centre Survey (diagram 1). It is also worth noting that some organizations apply with no intention or expectation of winning. What they expect to gain from the exercise is the feedback report, a key benefit to applicants for both American and European awards. All applicants receive a feedback report prepared by a team of experienced senior business managers from a variety of business sectors, who, having assessed the organization, present a balanced view of its strengths and areas for improvement in the format of a written report (see also Chapter 5).

"Self assessment, which every company ought to do anyway, is extremely revealing"
- Clive Jeanes, Managing Director of the European Division of Milliken, 1993 European Quality Award Winners.

Winners of the Malcolm Baldrige National Quality Award have indicated that the feedback from earlier, unsuccessful applications dramatically increased the pace of their improvement initiatives. Texas Instrument Defence Systems and Electronics Group, winners in 1992, declared that, even after a number of years of implementing quality improvements, their previous feedback reports from 'unsuccessful applications' moved them forward by the equivalent of two years in one.

2.6 Benefit 6: Self assessment to make inter divisional comparisons

Ranked last in the Bristol Quality Centre survey, this is when the result of the self assessments are used to compare, and possibly rank, interdivisional performance, i.e. to create a league table of performance.

The relevance of this activity probably depends on the culture of a business, and the benefits bring with them the common inherent dangers of creating league tables. Many will interprete this potential benefit as a potential danger. However, if used constructively, the assessments can allow each division of a large organization to progress using its own unique set of approaches and techniques, whilst at the same time the success and suitability of each division's approaches and techniques can be measured and compared with each other and relevant best practices can be shared (see also benefit 2.2.).

3 Using the measures as part of a strategic management framework

Using these advanced models of corporate excellence to evaluate your organization is obviously only one aspect of the entire self assessment process; and if the whole exercise ends there, then the major purpose of using these models has been wasted. Indeed, the main reason for using them should be to ensure that results initiate action to improve the performance of an organization.

However, before assessing how it is possible to use a corporate excellence model for strategic management and action-planning, or as the basis for improvement projects, it may first help to understand how strategic action planning has been applied in Western management, and what most organizations commonly percieve as the needs for the late 1990's.

In the 1980s, strategic plans concentrated mainly on (a) which markets the company should be in, (b) which products or services it should be supplying, and (c) how to get those products or services to the market; i.e. the distribution activity. Additionally, managements would consider such matters as acquisitions and disposals and the overall investment programme for the organization.

Now in the early 1990s, most organizations have swung away from action-plans based solely on such business activities. Instead, we have moved towards strategic plans based on more advanced corporate models. Issues such as leadership, people, the control of resources, the use of information within the organization and the way customer relationships are managed, have come to the fore. Thus a new set of underlying 'core values' has been created (see also Chapter 4).

The pendulum has swung away from the 'macho' ethos of the 1980s, when managers were absorbed by takeovers, acquisitions, and the sales of products and services, towards those softer issues which define how the business is actually run, rather than what it does.

In the development of strategic plans, most organizations believe it would be wise to strike a balance between both the aforementioned approaches - although this is rarely achieved in practice i.e., it is necessary to look not just at the 'hard' issues of what markets are being served, which services are being provided and what results are being achieved, but also at the 'soft' issues that will support the efficient and successful delivery of those activities, and build a healthy organization in the long term.

If organizations do not follow a balanced route there is a danger that, for instance, in applying only the early 1990s-style philosophy, we will develop organizations that become excellent and effective in delivering only variants of today's products and services to variants of today's market customers. In the process, the opportunity to make the big, and vital, structural changes in products, services, and in markets and customers, will be missed.

Given that strategic planning has to be a balance between these issues, one must ensure that the actual strategic planning around the outputs of assessments against corporate excellence models is not aimed simply at improving the perceived 'score' of the organization. Rather, it must be based on the needs of the organization at that stage in its development, and it must be sensitive to the market environment in which the company finds itself. Plans for the development and deployment of any self assessment process should recognize this need at an early stage.

It is thus essential that after a self assessment, some mechanism is used to generate priorities relevant to the immediate needs of that part of the organization under consideration. Action plans must address those activities and issues that would be of maximum use to the organization and the achievement of its strategic plans, rather than just to maximize the score against the corporate excellence model.

Action planning and its integration into a strategic management framework is dealt with further in Chapter 5 and Appendix 1.

4 What are the business benefits of the core values of award 'models'?

The ease of gaining acceptance of a corporate model for self assessment is of course entirely dependent on the potential value it will bring to you, your organization and your stakeholders.

Perhaps one of the reasons that award processes such as the European Quality Award and the Malcolm Baldrige National Quality Award are gaining acceptance is that their underlying core 'Quality' values and principles are commonly perceived as being beneficial and relevant to the development of most organizations in today's climate of competitive global markets, fast paced technological innovation, and rapidly-changing working practices.

To enable self assessment to be widely used and its output accepted requires that recognition of such benefits should be widely and accepted throughout the organization.

The common underpinning 'values' contained within the award schemes frameworks and measures are listed overleaf and linked to an analysis of the perceived importance obtained from a recent Bristol Quality Centre survey of EFQM members. Where publicly stated the value description (overleaf) is based on that of the award administrators, i.e., it is their description of the value and its underlying benefit.

An understanding of these commonly recognized values and their benefits is often of use when communicating and positioning the purpose and benefits of a 'self assessment' which measures progress towards their adoption/achievement.

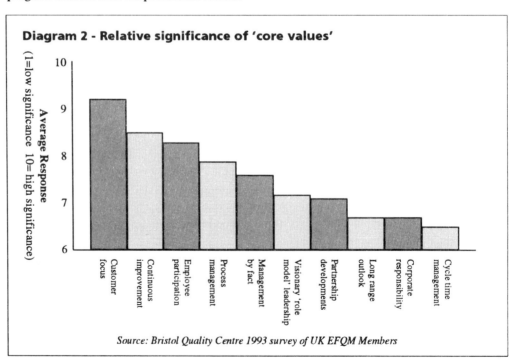

Diagram 2 - Relative significance of 'core values'

Source: Bristol Quality Centre 1993 survey of UK EFQM Members

4.1 Customer focus/customer driven quality

Customer-driven quality is a strategic concept. It is directed towards customer retention and market share gain. It demands constant sensitivity to emerging customer and market requirements, and measurement of the factors that drive customer satisfaction and retention. It also demands awareness of developments in technology, and rapid and flexible response to customer and market requirements.

Meeting or exceeding customer expectations not only delivers a one-off sale but also builds a 'perceived quality' image in the market place. Analysis of the 'Profit Impact of Market Strategies Database', (financial and strategic information on 3,000 businesses worldwide) has shown that perceived service quality is an important factor in business success. Results show that the leaders charge an average of almost ten per cent more for their products and services, increase their businesses twice as fast, and increase market share by an average of six per cent per year.

Additionally, customers are five times more likely to switch vendors because of perceived service problems than as a result of price concerns or 'product' quality issues. And since it costs five times as much to gain a new customer as it does to keep an existing one, it makes good financial sense to improve your processes and to take care of customers when they encounter problems. See also references 7,8,9,10 (appendix 2).

4.2 Continuous improvement

Achieving the highest levels of quality and competitiveness requires a well-defined and well-executed approach to continuous improvement. The term 'continuous improvement' refers to both incremental and 'breakthrough' improvement. A focus on improvement needs to be part of all operations and of all work units were a company. For many organizations the concept of continuous improvement can be epitomized by the Plan/Do/Check/Act concept as applied to either discrete problems, processes, or the organization as a whole i.e.

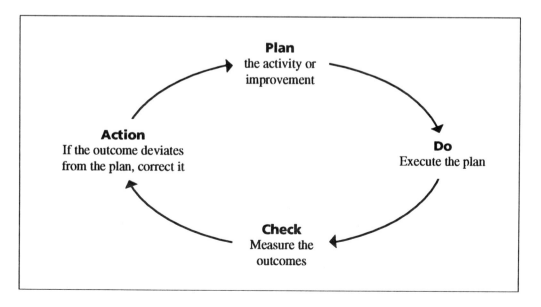

The approach to improvement needs to be 'embedded' in the way the organization functions. Embedded means that i) improvement is part of the daily work of all units; ii) improvement processes seek to elimate problems at their source; and iii) improvement is driven by opportunities to do better; as well as by problems that must be corrected.

We'll have to learn from the mistakes that others make. We can't live long enough to make them all ourselves.

- anon

Improvement should be driven not only by the objective to provide better product and service quality, but also by the need to be responsive and efficient - both conferring additional market place advantages.

4.3 Employee participation and development

An organization's success in meeting its quality and performance objectives depends increasingly on work-force quality and involvement. The close link between employee satisfaction and customer satisfaction creates a 'shared fate' relationship between companies and employees. For this reason, employee satisfaction measurement provides an important indicator of an organization's efforts to improve customer satisfaction and operating performance. Improving performance requires improvements at all levels. This, in turn, depends upon the skills and dedication of the entire work force. Organizations need to invest in the development of the work force and to seek new avenues to involve employees in improvement activities and decision making. Factors that bear upon the safety, health, well-being and morale of employees need to be part of the company's continuous improvement objectives. Increasingly, training and participation need to be tailored to a more diverse work force, and to more flexible work structures that encourage empowerment of all employees.

Tell me and I will forget

Show me and I will remember

Involve me and I will understand

- anon

Organizations can invest significantly in systems, technology, re-engineered processes and the like, but without the commitment, empowerment and involvement of their people, change is often slow.

4.4 Process management and 'preventive' improvement culture

The quality of any organization's products or services is determined by the basic business or operational processes that create them. If the chain of processes is made efficient and effective, then the resulting products or services will also be efficient and effective.

A process management approach enables managers to optimize the inter-relationships of functional organizations, to focus on the 'value-added' of all process elements and to adopt a preventive culture by emphasizing that continuous improvement and corrective action (action to eliminate the cause of an existing problem and to prevent its re-occurance) are goals at early stages in all processes.

Effort must therefore be directed primarily towards controlling the processes, rather than towards direct, specific controls of products or services or even worse of controlling people.

Applying direct product and service controls, such as inspection, often addresses only symptoms of potential problems, neglecting causes which lie within the process itself.

Concentrating on process management gives more efficient processes and lower costs. More effective processes produce high quality services, gain more satisfied customers and increase market share.

Note: A process is commonly defined as a means to add value to a series of inputs that provides an output that meets or exceeds the customer or user expectations.

4.5 Management by fact

Achievement of world class performance goals requires the use of reliable information and analysis to support, review and change beliefs, opinions, convictions and decisions. Facts needed for improvement and assessment can be gleaned from many aspects of an organization's activities including: customers; product and service performance; operations; market; competitive comparisons; suppliers; employees; and financial sources. Analysis may entail using data to reveal information - such as trends, projections, and cause and effect - that might not otherwise be evident. Facts and analysis should support a variety of company activities, such as planning, reviewing performance, improving operations, and comparing performance with that of competitors or with 'best practice' benchmarks.

"A wise man recognizes the convenience of a general statement but he bows to the authority of a particular fact."
- Oliver Wendell Holmes, SR., 1872

A major element in improving performance involves the creation and use of performance indicators. These are measurable characteristics of products, services, processes and operations, used by the company to evaluate and improve performance and to track progress. The indicators should be chosen to represent the factors that lead to improved customer satisfaction and operational performance. A system of indicators tied to customer and company performance requirements represents a clear and objective basis for aligning all activities of the company towards common goals. Through the analysis of data obtained in the tracking processes, the indicators themselves may be evaluated and changed over time.

4.6 Visionary 'role model' leadership

An organization's leaders must create a customer orientation, clear and visible quality values and high expectations. Reinforcement of the values and expectations requires substantial personal commitment and involvement. Leaders must take part in the creation of strategies, plans and systems for achieving excellence. Through regular personal involvement in visible activities, such as planning, communications, review of company quality performance, and recognizing employees for quality achievement, leaders serve as role models reinforcing the values and encouraging leadership in all levels of employee.

Managers: Manage within a paradigm
Leaders: Lead between paradigms
- anon

4.7 Partnership development

Organizations should seek to build internal and external partnerships to accomplish their overall goals. Fostering internal partnerships might involve the encouragement of employee cooperation through skills development, cross-training, or new work organizations, such as self directed work teams.

Examples of external partnerships could include those with competitors, customers, suppliers and educational organizations.

Partnerships should seek to develop longer-term objectives, and create a basis for mutual investments and growth. Partners should address the key requirements for success of the partnership, means of regular communication, approaches to evaluating progress, and the means for adapting to changing conditions.

4.8 Long-range outlook

Achieving long term quality and market leadership requires an organization to have a strong future orientation and a willingness to make long-term commitments to customers, employees, suppliers, stakeholders, and the community. Planning needs to determine or anticipate many types of changes including those that may affect customers' expectations of products and services, technological developments, changing customer segments, evolving regulatory requirements and community/social expectations, and thrusts by competitors. Plans, strategies, and resource allocations need to reflect these commitments and changes.

4.9 Corporate responsibility and impact on society

This 'value' relates to basic expectations the 'community' has of the organizations that serve it. Within organizations plans should exist to seek avenues to avoid problems, to measure 'societies' perception of the organization, to provide forthright company response if problems occur, and to make available information needed to maintain public awareness, safety, trust, and confidence.

Corporate citizenship requires the organization to take a leading role - within the reasonable limits of its resources - to address activities including education, resource conservation, support of community services, and the improvement of industry and business practices.

An effective organization should monitor the results, and number, of its approaches to 'corporate responsibility' and the ultimate perception of society on its 'impact on society'.

4.10 Cycle time management

Success in competitive markets increasingly demands ever-shorter cycles for new or improved product and service introduction. Faster and more flexible response to customers is of growing importance to operational management. Major improvements in response time often require work organizations, work processes and work paths to be simplified and shortened. To accomplish such improvement more attention should be given to measuring cycle time performance. This can be done by making response time a key indicator for work unit improvement processes. There are other important benefits to be derived from this focus: response time improvements often drive simultaneous improvements in organization, quality, and productivity. Hence it is often beneficial to consider response time, quality and productivity objectives together.

5 What's typically involved in doing it

5.1 Selecting a 'framework' to compare with

If you choose to self assess, you will achieve some or all of the benefits listed earlier in this book (see Chapter 2). To proceed you must first decide which framework for organizational excellence you wish to use to make your comparisons. Diagram 3 shows some essential attributes that should be considered when making a selection, some options that should be looked at, along with solutions that are commonly chosen and their advantages.

After reviewing your own needs and 'essential attributes' (see Diagram 3). You should read sections 5.1.1, 5.1.2, 5.1.3 and 5.1.4, which overviews the frameworks of three award schemes: The Deming Prize, The Malcolm Baldrige National Quality Award and the European Quality Award. We believe this process will help you come to a decision on which 'framework' to use.

Having decided on a framework we suggest that you proceed to section 5.2. and review which assessment process will be most appropriate for your organization as a method to make a comparison with your selected 'framework'.

Readers wishing to make a quick initial comparison should move to Chapter 6 which provides a starter kit based on the UK and European Quality Award process.

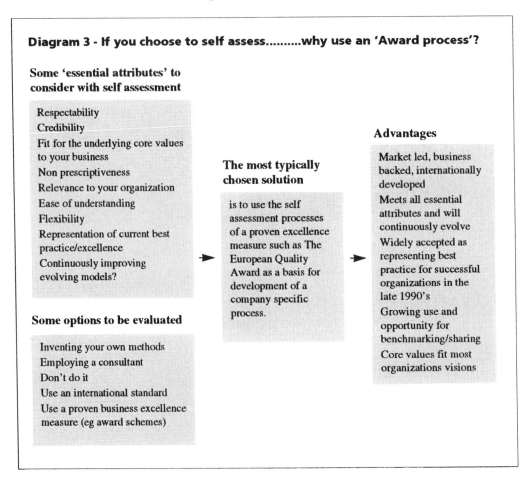

Diagram 3 - If you choose to self assess..........why use an 'Award process'?

Some 'essential attributes' to consider with self assessment

Respectability
Credibility
Fit for the underlying core values to your business
Non prescriptiveness
Relevance to your organization
Ease of understanding
Flexibility
Representation of current best practice/excellence
Continuously improving evolving models?

Some options to be evaluated

Inventing your own methods
Employing a consultant
Don't do it
Use an international standard
Use a proven business excellence measure (eg award schemes)

The most typically chosen solution

is to use the self assessment processes of a proven excellence measure such as The European Quality Award as a basis for development of a company specific process.

Advantages

Market led, business backed, internationally developed

Meets all essential attributes and will continuously evolve

Widely accepted as representing best practice for successful organizations in the late 1990's

Growing use and opportunity for benchmarking/sharing

Core values fit most organizations visions

5.1.1 The Deming Prize - A possible assessment framework?

In the early fifties the Deming Prize was established in Japan as a pre-eminent award for excellence in the implementation of concepts and techniques collectively then known as Total Quality Control (TQC). Although sometimes considered to be a Japanese oriented model of excellence, particularly with its emphasis on Statistical Quality Control, the Award has been won by two companies outside Japan. These winners were Florida Power and Light Company of USA and Philips in Taiwan. The effect of the Deming Prize in Japan has been to identify role models of Total Quality Control to inspire others to follow their path even though very few companies can ever hope to win the award.

While the Deming Prize audit framework is published (see below) the award process is not typically regarded as being sufficiently transparent to be used for self assessment. Its take-up in this mode is consequently low. The award is administered by the Japanese Union of Scientists and Engineers (JUSE) and applicants are not accepted unless they have been approved by the organization's own consultants, known as counsellors. For example, Florida Power and Light was counselled by JUSE for four years before being allowed to apply. While the assessment process is seen to be extremely vigorous, it is not clear how the judgements are made and what weighting is given to the various elements of the framework. Also, how assessors are trained to achieve a consistency of application of the framework is not made public and therefore is not readily transferable as an internal self assessment approach.

Audit Checklist for the Deming Application Prize

1. **Corporate Policy**

2. **Organization and Administration**

3. **Education and Dissemination**

4. **Implementation**
   To assure TQC, the following items must be checked:

i	Profit management	x	New product development
ii	Cost control	xi	Research management
iii	Purchasing and inventory control	xii	Vendor relations
iv	Production-process control	xiii	Grievance procedures
v	Facility management	xiv	Use of consumer information
vi	Instrumentation control	xv	QA (Quality Assurance)
vii	Personnel administration	xvi	Customer services
viii	Labour relations	xvii	Customer relations
ix	Education programmes		

   In particular, there is a check on systems in respect of:
   a. Collection and use of quality information
   b. Analysis
   c. Standardization
   d. Control
   e. Quality Assurance - how is the quality assurance system administered and diagnosed

5. **Effect**
   What impact has TQC's introduction had on quality, service, delivery, costs, profits, safety and the environment?

6. **For the Future**
   Are there plans to carry the TQC programme forward?

5.1.2 The Malcolm Baldrige National Quality Award - A possible assessment framework?

The principle of inspiring the business community by holding up role-models for them to emulate was taken up as a political initiative in the USA during the early eighties. In 1983 a White House Conference on Productivity was held including keynote speakers such as President Reagan, Vice-President Bush and Commerce Secretary Malcolm Baldrige. The report published from the conference opened with a very blunt headline statement: "America is the most productive nation in the world, but its growth in productivity has faltered. Some of the factors contributing to slower productivity growth are within our control and some are not, but it is important that we respond to this challenge." The report also highlighted the inter-relationship of improving quality, productivity and international competitiveness. The long and wide-ranging debate which then ensued resulted in agreement from both political and business leaders, that organizational excellence should be recognized by a highly prestigious national award made annually by the President. Thus, the Malcolm Baldrige National Quality Award was launched in 1988. The criteria for the award framework (see overleaf) were developed by learning from other models like the Deming Prize and in lengthy consultation with leaders in the business community. Not only did the criteria establish a consensus on business best practice but an annual review process was also established to ensure that it would continue to reflect current thinking on what constitutes a model of best practice.

One further significant step forward was the development of a clear assessment process against the framework (see overleaf) and a defined scoring approach against a weighted model. The benefit of this approach has not been just to lend credibility to the award process it has also opened up the framework for use as a self assessment tool within organizations striving for improved performance. The consistency of applying the framework within the award scheme and for self assessment has been achieved by the development of well-defined training programmes using calibrated case studies created from real business examples. The most powerful element of this process is the team consensus which is used to decide those applicants who will receive a site visit and ultimately provides a basis for selecting the winners. Bringing together the individual assessments of a team of senior managers ensures that their combined experience can be used to make a valuable judgement of the applicant's performance.

Baldrige Award Criteria Framework
Dynamic Relationships

```
                          System
                  ┌──────────────────┐
                  │   Management     │
                  │   of Process     │──►  ┌──────────────┐
                  │    Quality       │     │              │     Goal
                  │      5.0         │     │  Customer    │     ● Customer
                  ├──────────────────┤     │  Focus and   │     ● Satisfaction
         Driver   │   Human          │     │ Satisfaction │     ● Customer Satisfaction
                  │   Resource       │──►  │      7.0     │     ● Relative to Competitors
   ┌──────────┐   │   Development    │     └──────────────┘     ● Customer Retention
   │Leadership│◄─►│   and            │                          ● Market Share Gain
   │   1.0    │   │   Management     │
   └──────────┘   │      4.0         │     ┌──────────────┐
                  ├──────────────────┤     │  Quality and │     Measures of Progress
                  │   Strategic      │──►  │  Operational │     ● Product and Service
                  │   Quality        │     │   Results    │       Quality
                  │   Planning       │     │      6.0     │     ● Productivity
                  │      3.0         │     └──────────────┘       Improvement
                  ├──────────────────┤                          ● Waste Reduction/
                  │   Information    │                            Elimination
                  │   and Analysis   │                          ● Supplier Quality
                  │      2.0         │
                  └──────────────────┘
```

Award Criteria Framework

There are seven categories, as follows:

1.0 **Leadership**

2.0 **Information and Analysis**

3.0 **Strategic Quality Planning**

4.0 **Human Resource Development and Management**

5.0 **Management of Process Quality**

6.0 **Quality and Operational Results**

7.0 **Customer Focus and Satisfaction**

The framework connecting and integrating the categories is given in the figure above.

The framework has four basic elements:

Driver - Senior executive leadership creates the values, goals, and systems , and guides the sustained pursuit of customer value and company performance improvement.

Goal - The basic aim is the delivery of every-improving value to customers.

System - The System comprises of a set of well-defined and well-designed processes for meeting the company's customer, quality, and performance requirements.

Measures of Progress - Measures of progress provide a results-oriented basis for channelling actions to delivering ever-improving customer value and company performance.

The seven Criteria Categories shown in the figure are subdivided into 'Examination Items' and 'Areas to Address'.

Examination Items

There are 28 Examination Items, each focusing on a major management requirement.

Areas to Address

Each Examination Items consist of sets of Areas to Address (Areas). Information is submitted by applicants in response to specific requirements of these Areas.

For further information contact either NIST or BESAN (See Appendix 2)

Malcolm Baldrige Scoring Process

Either an 'Approach/Deployment' or a 'Results' judgement is applied to each framework 'item'

Score	Approach/Deployment
0%	● no systematic approach evident; anecdotal information
10% to 30%	● beginning of a systematic approach to the primary purposes of the Item ● early stages of a transition from reacting to problems to a general improvement orientation ● major gaps exist in deployment that would inhibit progress in achieving the primary purposes of the Item
40% to 60%	● a sound, systematic approach, responsive to the primary purposes of the Item ● a fact-based improvement process in place in key areas; more emphasis is placed on improvement than on reaction to problems ● no major gaps in deployment, though some areas or work units may be in very early stages of deployment
70% to 90%	● a sound, systematic approach, responsive to the overall purposes of the item ● a fact-based improvement process is a key management tool; clear evidence of refinement and improved integration as a result of improvement cycles and analysis ● approach is well-deployed, with no major gaps; deployment may vary in some areas or work units
100%	● a sound, systematic approach, fully responsive to all the requirements of the Item ● a very strong, fact-based improvement process is a key management tool; strong refinement and integration - backed by excellent analysis ● approach is fully deployed without any significant weaknesses or gaps in any areas or work units

Score	Results
0%	● no results or poor results in areas reported
10% to 30%	● early stages of developing trends; some improvements and/or early good performance levels in a few areas ● results not reported for many to most areas of importance to the applicant's key business requirements
40% to 60%	● improvement trends and/or good performance levels reported for many to most areas of importance to the applicant's key business requirements ● no pattern of adverse trends and/or poor performance levels in areas of importance to the applicant's key business requirements ● some trends and/or current performance levels - evaluated against relevant comparisons and/or benchmarks - show areas of strength and/or good to very good relative performance levels
70% to 90%	● current performance is good to excellent in most areas of importance to the applicant's key business requirements ● most improvement trends and/or performance levels are sustained ● many to most trends and/or current performance levels - evaluated against relevant comparisons and/or benchmarks - show areas of leadership and very good relative performance levels
100%	● current performance is excellent in most areas of importance to the applicant's key business requirements ● excellent improvement trends and/or sustained excellent performance levels in most areas ● strong evidence of industry and benchmark leadership demonstrated in many areas

Malcolm Baldrige National Quality Award - Key facts and figures

Between 1988 and 1992 there were approximately one million copies of the MBNQA application and guidelines documents distributed in the USA and with less than 500 applicants for the award, it is obvious that most of the copies are being used for self assessment rather than award application.

The toughness of the measures can be observed from an analysis of the scores obtained by those who felt they were good enough to apply to win the Malcolm Baldrige National Quality Award.

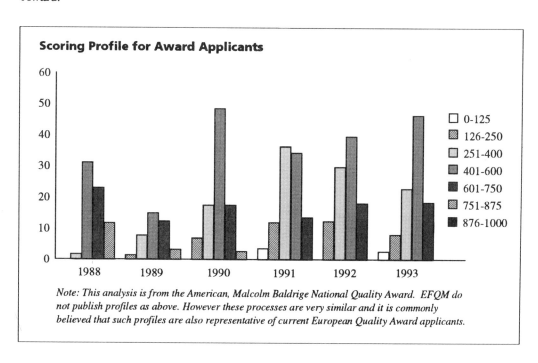

Note: This analysis is from the American, Malcolm Baldrige National Quality Award. EFQM do not publish profiles as above. However these processes are very similar and it is commonly believed that such profiles are also representative of current European Quality Award applicants.

Winners *(Malcolm Baldrige National Quality Award)*

The first Malcolm Baldrige National Quality Awards were presented by President Ronald Reagan in 1988. With 2 awards available in 3 categories (Service/Manufacturing/Small Business),the winners are:

1988

Manufacturing:	Motorola Inc.
	Westinghouse Commercial Fuels Division
Small Business:	Globe Metallurgical (ferroalloys and silicon metals/steel manufacturing)

1989

In 1989, awards were presented in only the manufacturing category

Milliken & Company

Xerox Business Products and Systems

1990

The first award in the service category was presented in 1990:

Service: Federal Express Corporation

Manufacturing: Cadillac Motor Car Company

IBM Rochester

Small Business: Wallace Co Inc. (distribution pipes/valves/fittings to oil and chemical industry)

1991

1991 was a year for electronics companies with awards going to:

Manufacturing: Solectron Corporation (printed circuit boards)

Zytec Corporation (electronic power supplies)

Small Business: Marlow Industries (thermoelectric coolers)

1992

5 out of the potentially available 6 awards were presented in 1992.

Manufacturing: AT&T Network Systems Group, Transmission Systems Business Unit

Texas Instruments Inc.,Defense Systems & Electronics Group

Service: AT&T Universal Card Services

The Ritz-Carlton Hotel Company

Small Business Granite Rock Company (rock, sand and gravel aggregates)

1993

In 1993 the awards were presented to:

Manufacturing: Eastman Chemical Company

Small Business: Ames Rubber Corporation

5.1.3 The European and UK Quality Awards - A possible assessment framework?

Just as the first Malcolm Baldrige National Quality Award annual cycle was being run in 1988, the European Foundation for Quality Management (EFQM) was being established. The EFQM defined its mission as 'to support the management of Western European companies in accelerating the process of making quality a decisive influence for achieving global competitive advantage'. With this aim in mind, they identified the achievements of award processes like the Deming Prize and the Malcolm Baldrige National Quality Award and established a recognition programme to develop a European-based equivalent. This programme, involving more than 200 pan-European organizations, resulted in the launch of the European Quality Award in 1992, incorporating a similar framework (see below and overleaf) to that used in the USA and with a very similar assessment and scoring process.

In developing this European model of Corporate Excellence, the EFQM wanted to ensure that it not only reflected current thinking on best practice measures but also included some vision of what a world class organization would be measuring and achieving in the future. To reach a consensus, there was a wide-ranging debate within the European business community to arrive at the model and the weightings within it. The result was a framework which had built in the strengths of its forerunners but added improvements with a distinctly European dimension.

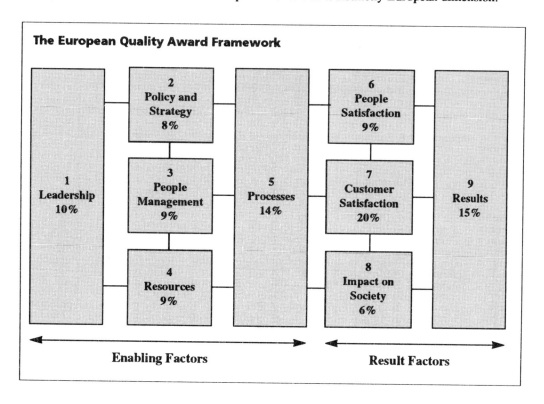

The European Quality Award Framework

	2 Policy and Strategy 8%		**6** People Satisfaction 9%	
1 Leadership 10%	**3** People Management 9%	**5** Processes 14%	**7** Customer Satisfaction 20%	**9** Results 15%
	4 Resources 9%		**8** Impact on Society 6%	

Enabling Factors   **Result Factors**

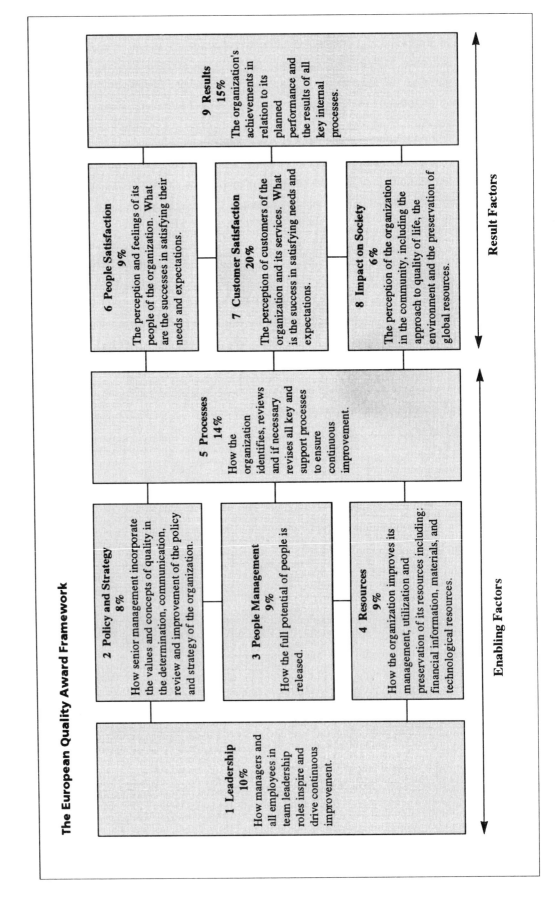

The European Quality Award Framework

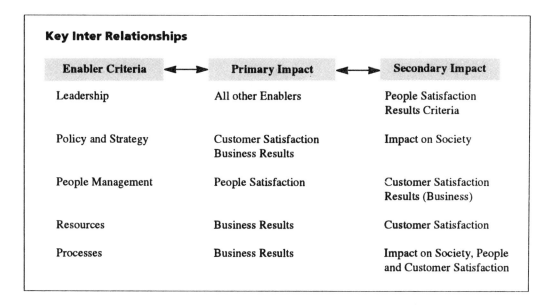

Key Inter Relationships

Enabler Criteria	Primary Impact	Secondary Impact
Leadership	All other Enablers	People Satisfaction Results Criteria
Policy and Strategy	Customer Satisfaction Business Results	Impact on Society
People Management	People Satisfaction	Customer Satisfaction Results (Business)
Resources	Business Results	Customer Satisfaction
Processes	Business Results	Impact on Society, People and Customer Satisfaction

Some of the commonly perceived improvements include:

a. establishing a 50/50 balance in the model between the **enablers**, which outline how an organization's activities are managed and optimized, and the **results**, which demonstrate the ongoing business improvement.

b. incorporating a Business Results criterion which looks for financial performance as well as operational measures of effectiveness.

c. focusing on some wider issues through the Impact on Society criterion which addresses not only environmental concerns but how an organization contributes to the community in which it operates.

d. being even less prescriptive in its framework than its USA counterpart and thus providing for a wider acceptance of the framework as being relevant to all organizations.

The 'enabler' criteria (1 to 5) are further sub-divided into 25 sub criteria for consideration (see also Chapter 6.3 which analyses each sub criteria in detail). Instructions are given as to the maximum score allowable for each criterion. Similarly detailed instructions are given on how to score each criteria along 2 of 4 scoring dimensions. These are either:

Chart 1 The Enablers

The Assessor scores each part of the Enablers criteria on the basis of the combination of two factors.

1. The degree of excellence of your approach
2. The degree of deployment of your approach

Approach	Score	Deployment
Anecdotal or non-value adding.	0%	Little effective usage.
Some evidence of soundly based approaches and prevention based systems. Subject to occasional review. Some areas of integration into normal operation.	25%	Applied to about one-quarter of the potential when considering all relevant areas and activities.
Evidence of soundly based systematic approaches and prevention based systems. Subject to regular review with respect to business effectiveness. Integration into normal operations and planning well established.	50%	Applied to about half the potential when considering all relevant areas and activities.
Clear evidence of soundly based systematic approaches and prevention based systems. Clear evidence of refinement and improved business effectiveness through review cycles. Good integration of approach into normal operations and planning.	75%	Applied to about three quarters of the potential when considering all relevant areas and activities.
Clear evidence of soundly based systematic approaches and prevention based systems. Clear evidence of refinement and improved business effectiveness through review cycles. Approach has become totally integrated into normal working patterns. Could be used as a role model for other organizations.	100%	Applied to full potential in all relevant areas and activities.

For both 'Approach' and 'Deployment', the Assessor may choose one of the five levels 0%, 25%, 50%, 75%, or 100% as presented in the chart, or interpolate between these values.

or:

Chart 2 The Results

The Assessor scores each part of the Enablers criteria on the basis of the combination of two factors.

1   The degree of excellence of your results
2.   The scope of your results

Results	Score	Scope
Anecdotal.	0%	Results address few relevant areas and activities.
Some results show positive trends. Some favourable comparisons with own targets.	25%	Results address some relevant areas and activities.
Many results show positive trends over at least 3 years. Favourable comparisons with own targets in many areas. Some comparisons with external organizations. Some results are caused by approach.	50%	Results address many relevant areas and activities.
Most results show strongly positive trends over at least 3 years. Favourable comparisons with own targets in most areas. Favourable comparisons with external organizations in many areas. Many results are caused by approach.	75%	Results address most relevant areas and activities.
Strongly positive trends in all areas over at least 5 years. Excellent comparisons with own targets and external organizations in most areas. 'Best in Class' in many areas of activity. Results are clearly caused by approach. Positive indication that leading position will be maintained.	100%	Results address all relevant areas and facets of the organization.

For both 'Results' and 'Scope', the Assessor may choose one of five levels 0%, 25%,

---

These scoring methods are further discussed in Appendix 3.

EFQM's own examiners have to attend, each year, a formal and testing training course which includes a practical case study. Examiners work on a voluntary basis and are typically executive managers.

The actual methodology pursued for the assessment is aimed to give great transparency and credibility to the award system. The process starts with the submission of detailed written reports by the applicant (of up to 75 pages). The applicant is encouraged to prepare the report against the detailed criteria parts. The submission is scored by several assessors (typically 4 to 6) and detailed comments are written (as strengths and 'areas for improvement') on each, to support the scoring. There is a detailed protocol to settle differences in scoring between the assessors - it is not just a question of averaging, the outcome is one of concensus. The concensus is achieved through a structured process.

The top scorers on this first round are then subjected to a site visit of nominally 4 to 6 people for between 1 to 5 days, to verify and clarify the original submission. Again there is a detailed protocol on how the assessors behave during the site visit. A major characteristic of this site visit is that they are directed towards the areas highlighted by the scoring of the first round, i.e. they are assessing whether they find the actual situation better or worse than the perception gained through the submitted report. Again precautions are taken to ensure that the reasoning behind the recommendations are recorded in order to obtain maximum transparency and credibility.

The leaders of the assessment teams then report back to a panel of Jurors (N.B. the Jurors do not score the company's report nor do they participate in site visits). The Jurors then make the final decisions.

All applicants, whether or not subjected to a site visit, receive a written feedback from the European Foundation for Quality Management on the assessment of their organization.

Applicants to pay a fee (approx 2000 ecu) for the assessment. For further details on EFQM see Appendix 2.

The UK Quality Award

1994 will see the launch of of a new UK Quality Award. Administered by the British Quality Foundation, (see Appendix 2) this award process will replicate that of the European Foundation for Quality Management using exactly the same model and assessment process. An order card for further information is contained in the appendices.

Some facts and figures *(The European Quality Award)*
1992

The first European Quality Award was presented on October 15, 1992, by His Majesty King Juan Carlos of Spain at the Palacia de Congresos in Madrid.

In this first Award year, the jurors selected four applicants to receive European Quality 'Prizes':

- BOC Limited, Special Gases

- Industrias de Ubierna SA - UBISA
- Milliken European Division
- Rank Xerox Limited

Rank Xerox Ltd was announced the outright winner.

1993

In the second year, 1993, four 'finalists' were announced, these are:

- Cablelettra SpA (Italy) (transportation equipment/rubber and plastics/electronic equipment)
- ICL Manufacturing Division
- Milliken European Division
- Varian-TEM Ltd

a 'prize' was presented to ICL Manufacturing Division
and
Milliken European Division was announced the 'award' winner.

5.1.4 Selecting a model

Having read and evaluated the process described in sections 5.1.1, 5.1.2 and 5.1.3, a key task is to select a framework for assessing your own organization. The European Quality Award and Malcolm Baldrige National Quality Award are both seen as excellent and robust models. In the end your choice will probably be driven by the location or the parentage of your organization: if you are based in the USA or have a strong USA parent organization then the MBNQA will probably be the most appropriate. For most organizations that are based in Europe the EQA or its national deravitives will be the most appropriate model as it will additionally allow for direct comparisons and benchmarking with other European based organizations. Both of these models are comparable in the scoring and in most cases a 500 point out of 1000 score on the EQA model will equate to a similar score on the MBNQA model. In the final analysis geographic location will probably be the determinant of the model to be used.

5.2 Developing a self assessment process

There are many processes available by which organizations can position themselves against a selected framework. These can range from simple questionnaires, tick-boxes and maturity grids through to complex and detailed methods of data collection and the production of reports.

To apply to win a prestigious award such as the European or UK Quality Award, an organization is allowed up to 75 pages to describe its performance and excellence. Some organizations choose this approach for their own internal self assessment, while others move only cautiously in this direction.

The figure below shows the steps of a typical self assessment process. To help you decide how to plan to address each step within your own organization, each activity is discussed further in sections 5.2.1 to 5.2.5 along with prompt questions that may aid your thinking. Frequent references are made to Appendix 1 where example processes are discussed. If you are seeking specific guidance or detailed methods, we suggest you read Appendix 1 first in order to understand the relative strengths of different self assessment processes. If you are looking for a quick initial process to get you started, we suggest you read Chapter 6 first.

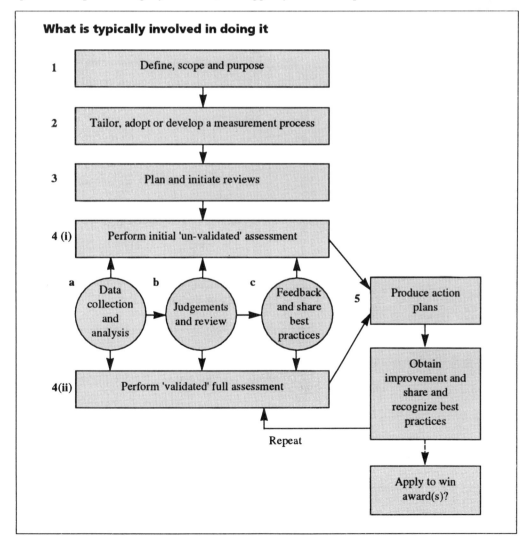

What is typically involved in doing it

1. Define, scope and purpose
2. Tailor, adopt or develop a measurement process
3. Plan and initiate reviews
4 (i) Perform initial 'un-validated' assessment

a. Data collection and analysis
b. Judgements and review
c. Feedback and share best practices

4(ii) Perform 'validated' full assessment

5. Produce action plans

Obtain improvement and share and recognize best practices

Repeat

Apply to win award(s)?

5.2.1. Step 1 - Defining Purpose and Scope

Issues to be addressed	Some options and points to consider
You will need to ask yourself what is the scope of your self assessment. For instance, is it the whole organization, specific divisions or perhaps discrete departments? How will this evolve over time?	When drawing a 'ring-fence' around a part of your organization, ask yourself: i) will the feedback and output be in a format that is useful for that part of the organization being assessed? ii) can you usefully apply all of the criteria within the 'ring-fence'? For instance, who are the customers, what are the key processes and what are the key business results?
You need also to define the purpose for which you are undertaking the self assessment. For example, are you doing it because you wish to measure, target and direct improvements as highlighted in Chapter 2.1? Or are you intending to apply for, and/or to win an award at some future date? Does one lead to the other?	Are your aims appropriately stretching? When defining your key purpose for self assessment ask yourself how this approach and model will be seen to align with current and past quality and improvement related initiatives. If you intend at some point to apply to win an award, you should consider the need to back-plan this from your intended date of application. You should also bear in mind the pre-requisite that, prior to application, you will need to be describing the excellence of your business in a 75-page document.
What will you do with the output?	Is the output confidential? How will your output be aligned to your business planning cycles (see also Step 5)? Is the output just for the executive team or will it be released to other employees?

5.2.2 Step 2 - Adopting a measurement process

Issues to be addressed	Some options and points to consider

Are you able to use any of the commonly used methods of conducting self assessment described in Appendix 1 and Step 4 overleaf?
 	
E.g.- the 'Award Style reports'
   - the Facilitator Led Workshop
   - Questionnaires or Checklist
   - 'Hybrid' approach
	Most organizations use different methods of data collection (see Appendix 1) but base their 'scoring' processes on that of the award scheme (see Appendix 3).

Can you adopt, unchanged, the framework and scoring process of say the European Quality Award for your comparisons?	Assess carefully the added-value of changing a recognized model. One advantage of aligning totally to say the European Quality Award framework is that, in so doing, you take a strategic decision that it will be the model of corporate excellence for your organization. In making this decision you are effectively getting your 'renewal' for free, since, each year, the EFQM and the executive managers who help deploy the process for them are reviewing and improving the excellence model.
Do you believe that you need to tailor the model or process e.g. the words of the award framework - to suit your organization?	At a detailed level, many organizations enhance the understanding and useability of the model by using their own terminology at the detailed 'areas to address' level i.e. the meaning of the European Quality Award assessment structure remains unchanged but added value is created by using company specific jargon, terminology and examples.

5.2.3 Step 3 - Planning and initiating reviews

Issues to be addressed	Some options and points to consider
What will be the frequency of the reviews? Will the assessment be voluntary or compulsory?	Many organizations operate on annual cycles.
Can a business unit initiate a review itself or must it wait for a corporate review process?	Many organizations perform 'validated assessments' by drawing on a trained pool of executive managers' to assist the process, i.e. executive managers are part of a judgement and feedback process that may 'validate' a business unit's self or 'un-validated' analysis (see also Step 4b overleaf). If you use this approach, consider also having a simpler 'un-validated' process that individual business units can self apply. This can help manage expectations and unite unit executives prior to the undertaking of a full review. See 'Award style process' and 'Hybrid approaches' in Appendix 1 for further explanation.

5.2.4 Step 4 - Performing validated/un-validated assessments

Issues to be assessed	Some options and points to consider
A) Data Collection This means ensuring that your assessment is based on facts not guesswork. Options include: - written submissions to assessors; - proforma's or pre-formatting of existing business results by the unit; - supply of pre-formatted results followed by site visits to sample the pervasiveness and success of the approaches to the enablers; - questionnaires; - interviews; - focus groups; - simply perceptions, or views expressed, by an executive or other team. Appendix 1 provides additional information.	Consider having a process that ensures that the assessed business owns, creates or agrees the data collection plan to produce the data by which it is judged. Consider simpler processes such as perceptions and views expressed by executives and/or questionnaires and proforma's for un-validated processes. But recognize that, for a validated full assessment, you may wish to capture a pack of information/data that will ensure a fact based judgement and can be re-visited and used when reassessments are undertaken.
B) Judgement This means ensuring that your assessment determines the 'best estimate' of your current position and has high acceptance from the assessed business. - a typical approach is to use a team of up to six trained assessors from outside the unit being assessed. Note: The managers involved usually value such a commitment as an important and ongoing part of their personal development;	Consider having a code of ethics by which assessors operate and whether they do, or do not, disclose information. In addition, consider having a pass-fail training course for your assessors. Assessor should exhibit a balanced profile of operation-wide management skills, communication, interpersonal skills, knowledge of the model, the assessment process being used and be neither excessively optimistic or pessimistic in their scoring assessment.

- consider your needs for 'moderation', i.e. do you need external support to help you 'calibrate' your scores to that of the EFQM?	The assessment 'calibration' to the model can easily be obtained by using the same training processes as those employed for the real award assessors. These courses use case studies and can be delivered within three days. (See Appendix 2) - consider whether you need a corporate resource, if not an external resource, to help ensure consistency between your internal assessments.
- how will you manage under- or overly-optimistic scoring?	- consider the advantages of having 'home' and 'away' assessors, i.e. home assessors coming from the unit being assessed, away assessors coming from elsewhere in the organization.
C) Feedback What will you do with the results? Are the numbers confidential? Is the analysis of strength and areas for improvement confidential? How will the feedback be presented to the unit?	You should be careful to ensure that the style of the assessment and scoring does not become overly 'audit' based. i.e. The focus should be on the identification of strengths and areas for improvement, supported by a consensus score. Do not let the assessors slip into a consultancy role. Concentrate on keeping the feedback report as a clear and precise identification of both strengths and areas for improvement rather than 'helpful' advice on 'what to do next'. Most organizations separate the feedback, that is 'where are we now' from the action planning - 'what should we do next'. Mixing these two phases is a common error which only causes confusion and weakens the opportunities that the self assessment process presents. Consider the option of having internal awards or other recognition processes to recognize either the highest scoring or the fastest changing parts of your organization.

5.2.5 Step 5 - Producing action plans

Issue to be addressed	Some options and points to consider
What will you do with the output of an assessment?	Consider having a process that aids the assessed activity to identify, from the many strengths and areas for improvement presented to it, a focus on what are key business issues to be addressed within any particular time-frame. Consider moving towards making the production of an action plan a 'mandatory pre-requisite' of obtaining or having support to undertake a review. Consider having the timing of the assessments aligned to, or perhaps even totally integrated within, the annual business planning cycles.

6 A 'starter' kit

6.1 Objective

Many executive managers appreciate the potential benefits obtainable from 'self assessment', but are bewildered by the range of opportunities presented to them as options to move forward.

An increasingly common starting point is the use of an executive scoring workshop. The purpose of such a workshop is to enable a team of senior managers to assess their organization against an internationally recognized model of excellence, in the example we shall use - the European Quality Award (EQA) - thereby evaluating the potential of the model to identify perceived strengths and areas for improvement within their organization.

Within one or two days, the process described below (6.2) can create a picture of an organization, generate a set of 'scores' that profile its achievements against the EQA framework, and provide the basis to evaluate how further, or more detailed, application of the EQA process can be of use.

Note:-

Further details of this and other more detailed methods are provided in Appendix 1. The intent of this chapter is to provide a process to start with.

Readers may use this process to undertake a scoring workshop (see 6.2 below) or may, equally, benefit from simple self scoring, using the proformas (6.3 overleaf) as a vehicle to record their own thoughts and thereby obtain an increased understanding of the EQA model.

6.2 Background and preparation for a scoring workshop

For readers wishing to use the proformas (6.3) to prepare for a scoring workshop, we recommend the following process:

Step 1 Pre-briefing and Pre-work

Participants complete the steps listed in the analysis overleaf (6.3) and list their own perceptions of importance, and perceived strengths/areas for improvement of the organization being assessed, when compared to the criteria on pages 41 to 116.

This activity will typically take 4 to 6 hours, and should result in a score being allocated by one of the methods described in Appendix 3.

Step 2 Workshop

Participants attend a two day 'scoring workshop'.

We recommend commencing on the evening of day one, with an introductory session followed by an 8 to 10 hour workshop on the subsequent day.

The workshop should be led by two managers trained in the European Quality Award assessment processes and scoring (see Appendix 3).

A typical workshop process consists of sequentially following the steps below:

i)   Introduce the criteria to be scored (using the material overleaf) and discuss views and scores on relative importance (step 1 on the proforma's).

ii) 'Brainstorm' perceived strengths and areas for improvement.
     -   participants use their pre-prepared notes.
     -   one of the facilitators captures delegates' 'strengths' on a flip chart.
     -   the other facilitator captures areas for improvement on a second 'flip chart'.

iii) Facilitators test and agree the flip chart 'analysis' of 'strengths' and 'areas for improvement' with the delegates.

iv) Facilitators lead participants into scoring.

v)   Participants score as individuals.

vi) Individuals scores are shared, possible differences in views analysed and a consensus obtained.

'Warning' to be successful with steps iv) and vi) it is important to recognize that some basic skills in scoring will be needed by the facilitators. These can be obtained through the assessor training courses. This book alone cannot brief and train the facilitator. This text is intended to prepare the participants.

Step 3   How to use the output
The workshop output will help you to identify your current strengths and areas for improvement. This can be a very valuable short term planning aid. We recommend that the flip charts are typed and used for subsequent review and action planning.

Additionally, and equally importantly, those involved will have been able to assess the process as a whole, and to evaluate more fully its potential benefits.

We strongly suggest that your participants diary an additional day, after the scoring workshop, on which they will analyse the output from the first workshop, assess underlying themes and agree future plans.

6.3 Analysis proformas

Completion of the following proformas will provide both briefing for a scoring workshop and a method by which individuals can increase their knowledge and understanding of the EQA model.

The proformas for each criterion overleaf consists of:-

i) an introduction, i.e. a graphical overview of the sub criteria contained within each criterion, e.g. for Criterion 1, the graphical overview shows the relationship of subcriteria 1a to 1f, and

ii) a series of analysis sheets for each sub criteria that will enable the reader to capture their own thoughts on performance.

Note:-

- we recommend using the scoring cards from Appendix 3 to 'score' each sub criteria after you have completed the steps overleaf.

Criterion 1 - Leadership

This criterion looks at how managers drive the organization towards the achievement of organizational excellence. The next 12 pages will help to capture your views on 1a to 1f.

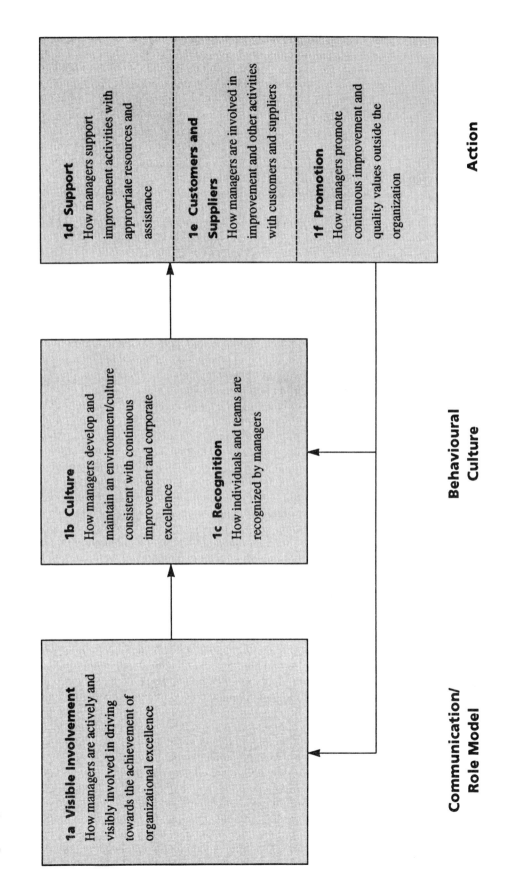

1a Visible Involvement
How managers are actively and visibly involved in driving towards the achievement of organizational excellence

1b Culture
How managers develop and maintain an environment/culture consistent with continuous improvement and corporate excellence

1c Recognition
How individuals and teams are recognized by managers

1d Support
How managers support improvement activities with appropriate resources and assistance

1e Customers and Suppliers
How managers are involved in improvement and other activities with customers and suppliers

1f Promotion
How managers promote continuous improvement and quality values outside the organization

Communication/ Role Model

Behavioural Culture

Action

Leadership 1a

This criterion involves an assessment of how the executive team and all of the managers inspire and drive the business towards organizational excellence

1a How visible involvement is achieved

Areas to address could include:

How managers act as role models and lead by example.

How managers participate in training and development activities.

How managers demonstrate commitment to the organization's quality values and goals.

How managers make themselves accessible and listen to staff.

How managers and leaders communicate with staff.

Step 1. Assess importance of criterion

	These are not key issues	These issues are moderately important	These issues are important	These issues are critical
	(0)	(1)	(2)	(3)
Importance Rating				

Note: Tick a box to indicate your view of the importance of this criterion (note, the description of the criterion is the words after 1a)

Step 2. Detail your overall process

Note: List the overall process you use to manage all the activities related to this criterion

Step 3. List specific policies, processes and practices

Step 4. For each activity listed in step 3 list how long you have been using each policy, process or practice (years/months)

Step 5. List to what extent you want to deploy each policy, process and practice and how far they have been deployed to date (e.g. by site, organizational level, department, activity, product etc.)

Step 6. List how and how often you review the effectiveness of each activity and the overall process.

Note: Annotate your comments onto the list from Step 3

Step 7. List improvements resulting from reviews

Step 8. Review your comments on steps 1 to 7 as a whole, and form and record an opinion on the success of the approaches used and their deployment. List this as a set of composite perceived strengths and areas for improvement. The scoring card in Appendix 3 should be used to help your thoughts. In arriving at your assessment consider the basis for, and proven effectiveness of, the approaches that have been deployed.

Perceived strengths (+)	Perceived areas for improvement (-)

Note: List also as areas for improvement relevant activities that you feel should be initiated and are not at present undertaken.

This criterion involves an assessment of how the executive team and all of the managers inspire and drive the business towards organizational excellence

Leadership 1b

1b How a consistent quality "culture" is obtained

Areas to address could include:

How managers demonstrate actions and behaviours consistent with the organization's quality values and strategies.

How managers are involved in assessing progress and awareness of quality goals, values and strategies.

How commitment to and achievement of such goals is recognized in the appraisal and promotion of staff at all levels.

How feedback and behavioural monitoring is used to review leadership and management behaviours.

Step 1. Assess importance of criterion

	These are not key issues	These issues are moderately important	These issues are important	These issues are critical
Importance Rating	(0)	(1)	(2)	(3)

Note: Tick a box to indicate your view of the importance of this criterion (note, the description of the criterion is the words after 1b)

Step 2. Detail your overall process

Note: List the overall process you use to manage all the activities related to this criterion

Step 3. List specific policies, processes and practices

44

Step 4. For each activity listed in step 3 list how long you have been using each policy, process or practice (years/months)

Step 5. List to what extent you want to deploy each policy, process and practice and how far they have been deployed to date (e.g. by site, organizational level, department, activity, product etc.)

Step 6. List how and how often you review the effectiveness of each activity and the overall process.

Note: Annotate your comments onto the list from Step 3

Step 7. List improvements resulting from reviews

Step 8. Review your comments on steps 1 to 7 as a whole, and form and record an opinion on the success of the approaches used and their deployment. List this as a set of composite perceived strengths and areas for improvement. The scoring card in Appendix 3 should be used to help your thoughts. In arriving at your assessment consider the basis for, and proven effectiveness of, the approaches that have been deployed.

Perceived strengths (+)

Perceived areas for improvement (-)

Note: List also as areas for improvement relevant activities that you feel should be initiated and are not at present undertaken.

Leadership 1c

This criterion involves an assessment of how the executive team and all of the managers inspire and drive the business towards organizational excellence

1c How timely recognition and appreciation of the efforts and successes of individuals and teams is undertaken

Areas to address could include:

How managers are involved in the recognition of success at different organizational and geographic levels and locations.

How such recognition is provided outside the organization for example with customers and suppliers.

How such approaches are reviewed for their effectiveness and improved.

Step 1. Assess importance of criterion

	These are not key issues	These issues are moderately important	These issues are important	These issues are critical
Importance Rating	(0)	(1)	(2)	(3)

Note: Tick a box to indicate your view of the importance of this criterion (note, the description of the criterion is the words after 1c)

Step 2. Detail your overall process

Note: List the overall process you use to manage all the activities related to this criterion

Step 3. List specific policies, processes and practices

46

Step 4. For each activity listed in step 3 list how long you have been using each policy, process or practice (years/months)

Step 5. List to what extent you want to deploy each policy, process and practice and how far they have been deployed to date (e.g. by site, organizational level, department, activity, product etc.)

Step 6. List how and how often you review the effectiveness of each activity and the overall process.

Note: Annotate your comments onto the list from Step 3

Step 7. List improvements resulting from reviews

Step 8. Review your comments on steps 1 to 7 as a whole, and form and record an opinion on the success of the approaches used and their deployment. List this as a set of composite perceived strengths and areas for improvement. The scoring card in Appendix 3 should be used to help your thoughts. In arriving at your assessment consider the basis for, and proven effectiveness of, the approaches that have been deployed.

Perceived strengths (+)	Perceived areas for improvement (-)

Note: List also as areas for improvement relevant activities that you feel should be initiated and are not at present undertaken.

This criterion involves an assessment of how the executive team and all of the managers inspire and drive the business towards organizational excellence

Leadership 1d

1d Support by the provision of appropriate resources and assistance

Areas to address could include:

How resources and assistance for improvement activities are appropriately prioritized at different organizational levels.

How learning, facilitation and improvement activities are funded.

How those taking part in quality activities are actively supported.

How staff are released from other commitments to participate in improvement activities.

Step 1. Assess importance of criterion

	These are not key issues	These issues are moderately important	These issues are important	These issues are critical
Importance Rating	(0)	(1)	(2)	(3)

Note: Tick a box to indicate your view of the importance of this criterion (note, the description of the criterion is the words after 1d)

Step 2. Detail your overall process

Note: List the overall process you use to manage all the activities related to this criterion

Step 3. List specific policies, processes and practices

Step 4. For each activity listed in step 3 list how long you have been using each policy, process or practice (years/months)

Step 5. List to what extent you want to deploy each policy, process and practice and how far they have been deployed to date (e.g. by site, organizational level, department, activity, product etc.)

Step 6. List how and how often you review the effectiveness of each activity and the overall process.

Note: Annotate your comments onto the list from Step 3

Step 7. List improvements resulting from reviews

Step 8. Review your comments on steps 1 to 7 as a whole, and form and record an opinion on the success of the approaches used and their deployment. List this as a set of composite perceived strengths and areas for improvement. The scoring card in Appendix 3 should be used to help your thoughts. In arriving at your assessment consider the basis for, and proven effectiveness of, the approaches that have been deployed.

Perceived strengths (+)

Perceived areas for improvement (-)

Note: List also as areas for improvement relevant activities that you feel should be initiated and are not at present undertaken.

This criterion involves an assessment of how the executive team and all of the managers inspire and drive the business towards organizational excellence

Leadership 1e

1e How customers and suppliers are involved

Areas to address could include:

How managers take positive steps to meet, understand and respond to the needs of customers and suppliers.

How joint improvement activities with customers and suppliers are established and participated in.

How managers are involved in establishing and participating in partnerships with customers and suppliers.

Step 1. Assess importance of criterion

	These are not key issues	These issues are moderately important	These issues are important	These issues are critical
Importance Rating	(0)	(1)	(2)	(3)

Note: Tick a box to indicate your view of the importance of this criterion (note, the description of the criterion is the words after 1e)

Step 2. Detail your overall process

Note: List the overall process you use to manage all the activities related to this criterion

Step 3. List specific policies, processes and practices

Step 4. For each activity listed in step 3 list how long you have been using each policy, process or practice (years/months)

Step 5. List to what extent you want to deploy each policy, process and practice and how far they have been deployed to date (e.g. by site, organizational level, department, activity, product etc.)

Step 6. List how and how often you review the effectiveness of each activity and the overall process.

Note: Annotate your comments onto the list from Step 3

Step 7. List improvements resulting from reviews

Step 8. Review your comments on steps 1 to 7 as a whole, and form and record an opinion on the success of the approaches used and their deployment. List this as a set of composite perceived strengths and areas for improvement. The scoring card in Appendix 3 should be used to help your thoughts. In arriving at your assessment consider the basis for, and proven effectiveness of, the approaches that have been deployed.

Perceived strengths (+)

Perceived areas for improvement (-)

Note: List also as areas for improvement relevant activities that you feel should be initiated and are not at present undertaken.

This criterion involves an assessment of how the executive team and all of the managers inspire and drive the business towards organizational excellence

Leadership 1f

1f How active promotion of quality management outside the business is undertaken

Areas to address could include:

How policies are established to give direction for the promotion of quality management outside the organization.

How managers, as a result of those policies, actively promote quality management for example membership of professional bodies, publication of booklets, presentation of conferences, articles, support in the local community etc.

Step 1. Assess importance of criterion

	These are not key issues	These issues are moderately important	These issues are important	These issues are critical
Importance Rating	(0)	(1)	(2)	(3)

Note: Tick a box to indicate your view of the importance of this criterion (note, the description of the criterion is the words after 1f)

Step 2. Detail your overall process

Note: List the overall process you use to manage all the activities related to this criterion

Step 3. List specific policies, processes and practices

Step 4. For each activity listed in step 3 list how long you have been using each policy, process or practice (years/months)

Step 5. List to what extent you want to deploy each policy, process and practice and how far they have been deployed to date (e.g. by site, organizational level, department, activity, product etc.)

Step 6. List how and how often you review the effectiveness of each activity and the overall process.

Note: Annotate your comments onto the list from Step 3

Step 7. List improvements resulting from reviews

Step 8. Review your comments on steps 1 to 7 as a whole, and form and record an opinion on the success of the approaches used and their deployment. List this as a set of composite perceived strengths and areas for improvement. The scoring card in Appendix 3 should be used to help your thoughts. In arriving at your assessment consider the basis for, and proven effectiveness of, the approaches that have been deployed.

Perceived strengths (+)	Perceived areas for improvement (-)

Note: List also as areas for improvement relevant activities that you feel should be initiated and are not at present undertaken.

You have now completed Criterion 1 - Note any actions required.

Criterion 2 - Policy and Strategy

This criterion looks at your Mission, Vision, Values and Strategies and how you plan to achieve them. The next 10 pages will help you to capture your views on 2a to 2e.

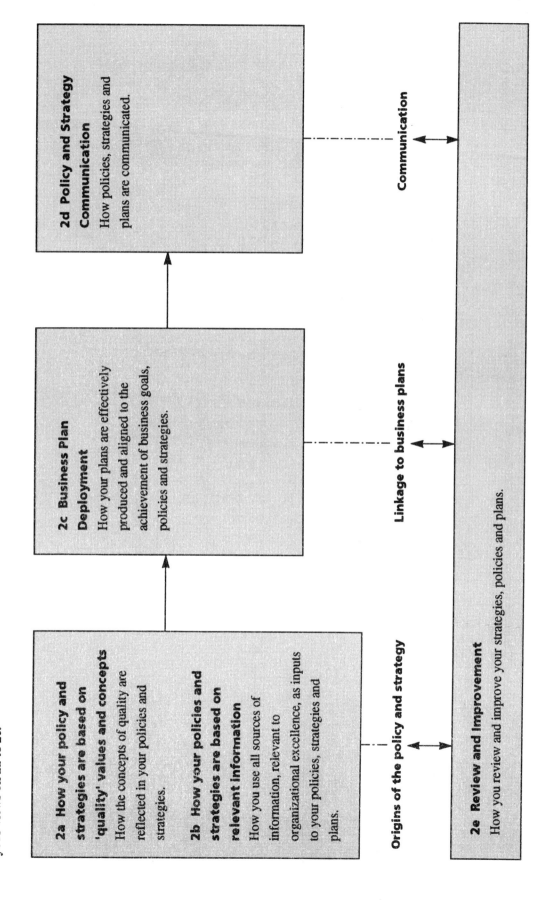

2a How your policy and strategies are based on 'quality' values and concepts
How the concepts of quality are reflected in your policies and strategies.

2b How your policies and strategies are based on relevant information
How you use all sources of information, relevant to organizational excellence, as inputs to your policies, strategies and plans.

2c Business Plan Deployment
How your plans are effectively produced and aligned to the achievement of business goals, policies and strategies.

2d Policy and Strategy Communication
How policies, strategies and plans are communicated.

Origins of the policy and strategy

Linkage to business plans

Communication

2e Review and Improvement
How you review and improve your strategies, policies and plans.

This criterion involves an assessment of the organization's mission, values, vision and strategic direction and the ways in which it achieves them.

Policy and Strategy 2a

2a How the concepts of quality and continuous improvement are incorporated into policy and strategies

Areas to address could include:

How such concepts and values are reflected in the organization's mission, vision, values and strategy statements.

How 'improvement' is seen to underpin all elements of policy and strategy.

Step 1. Assess importance of criterion

	These are not key issues	These issues are moderately important	These issues are important	These issues are critical
Importance Rating	(0)	(1)	(2)	(3)

Note: Tick a box to indicate your view of the importance of this criterion (note, the description of the criterion is the words after 2a)

Step 2. Detail your overall process

Note: List the overall process you use to manage all the activities related to this criterion

Step 3. List specific policies, processes and practices

Step 4. For each activity listed in step 3 list how long you have been using each policy, process or practice (years/months)

Step 5. List to what extent you want to deploy each policy, process and practice and how far they have been deployed to date (e.g. by site, organizational level, department, activity, product etc.)

Step 6. List how and how often you review the effectiveness of each activity and the overall process.

Note: Annotate your comments onto the list from Step 3

Step 7. List improvements resulting from reviews

Step 8. Review your comments on steps 1 to 7 as a whole, and form and record an opinion on the success of the approaches used and their deployment. List this as a set of composite perceived strengths and areas for improvement. The scoring card in Appendix 3 should be used to help your thoughts. In arriving at your assessment consider the basis for, and proven effectiveness of, the approaches that have been deployed.

Perceived strengths (+)

Perceived areas for improvement (-)

Note: List also as areas for improvement relevant activities that you feel should be initiated and are not at present undertaken.

This criterion involves an assessment of the organization's mission, values, vision and strategic direction and the ways in which it achieves them.

Policy and Strategy 2b

2b How information relevant to quality and continuous improvement is used in determining policy and strategies.

Areas to address could include:

How feedback from customers and suppliers is used.

How feedback from the company's employees is used e.g. survey and satisfaction data.

How benchmark data on performance with competitors and best in class organizations is used.

How external key indicators are used e.g. social, regulatory and legislative indicators, information and trends.

Step 1. Assess importance of criterion

	These are not key issues	These issues are moderately important	These issues are important	These issues are critical
	(0)	(1)	(2)	(3)
Importance Rating				

Note: Tick a box to indicate your view of the importance of this criterion (note, the description of the criterion is the words after 2b)

Step 2. Detail your overall process

Note: List the overall process you use to manage all the activities related to this criterion

Step 3. List specific policies, processes and practices

Step 4. For each activity listed in step 3 list how long you have been using each policy, process or practice (years/months)

Step 5. List to what extent you want to deploy each policy, process and practice and how far they have been deployed to date (e.g. by site, organizational level, department, activity, product etc.)

Step 6. List how and how often you review the effectiveness of each activity and the overall process.

Note: Annotate your comments onto the list from Step 3

Step 7. List improvements resulting from reviews

Step 8. Review your comments on steps 1 to 7 as a whole, and form and record an opinion on the success of the approaches used and their deployment. List this as a set of composite perceived strengths and areas for improvement. The scoring card in Appendix 3 should be used to help your thoughts. In arriving at your assessment consider the basis for, and proven effectiveness of, the approaches that have been deployed.

Perceived strengths (+)

Perceived areas for improvement (-)

Note: List also as areas for improvement relevant activities that you feel should be initiated and are not at present undertaken.

This criterion involves an assessment of the organization's mission, values, vision and strategic direction and the ways in which it achieves them.

Policy and Strategy 2c

2c How policy and strategies form the basis of business plans

Areas to address could include:

How business and local plans are tested, evaluated, approved and aligned to organizational policy and strategy.

How consistency between functional plans is ensured.

How resources are prioritized and allocated to plans.

Step 1. Assess importance of criterion

	These are not key issues	These issues are moderately important	These issues are important	These issues are critical
Importance Rating	(0)	(1)	(2)	(3)

Note: Tick a box to indicate your view of the importance of this criterion (note, the description of the criterion is the words after 2c)

Step 2. Detail your overall process

Note: List the overall process you use to manage all the activities related to this criterion

Step 3. List specific policies, processes and practices

Step 4. For each activity listed in step 3 list how long you have been using each policy, process or practice (years/months)

Step 5. List to what extent you want to deploy each policy, process and practice and how far they have been deployed to date (e.g. by site, organizational level, department, activity, product etc.)

Step 6. List how and how often you review the effectiveness of each activity and the overall process.

Note: Annotate your comments onto the list from Step 3

Step 7. List improvements resulting from reviews

Step 8. Review your comments on steps 1 to 7 as a whole, and form and record an opinion on the success of the approaches used and their deployment. List this as a set of composite perceived strengths and areas for improvement. The scoring card in Appendix 3 should be used to help your thoughts. In arriving at your assessment consider the basis for, and proven effectiveness of, the approaches that have been deployed.

Perceived strengths (+)

Perceived areas for improvement (-)

Note: List also as areas for improvement relevant activities that you feel should be initiated and are not at present undertaken.

This criterion involves an assessment of the organization's mission, values, vision and strategic direction and the ways in which it achieves them.

Policy and Strategy 2d

2d How policy and strategies are communicated

Areas to address could include:

How appropriate media are selected and used.

The effectiveness of specific processes used such as meetings, newsletters, posters, videos etc.

How the effectiveness of the communications of policy and strategy are evaluated and improved.

The overall communications plan and how it is prioritized for policy and strategy issues.

Step 1. Assess importance of criterion

	These are not key issues	These issues are moderately important	These issues are important	These issues are critical
	(0)	(1)	(2)	(3)
Importance Rating				

Note: Tick a box to indicate your view of the importance of this criterion (note, the description of the criterion is the words after 2d)

Step 2. Detail your overall process

Note: List the overall process you use to manage all the activities related to this criterion

Step 3. List specific policies, processes and practices

Step 4. For each activity listed in step 3 list how long you have been using each policy, process or practice (years/months)

Step 5. List to what extent you want to deploy each policy, process and practice and how far they have been deployed to date (e.g. by site, organizational level, department, activity, product etc.)

Step 6. List how and how often you review the effectiveness of each activity and the overall process.

Note: Annotate your comments onto the list from Step 3

Step 7. List improvements resulting from reviews

Step 8. Review your comments on steps 1 to 7 as a whole, and form and record an opinion on the success of the approaches used and their deployment. List this as a set of composite perceived strengths and areas for improvement. The scoring card in Appendix 3 should be used to help your thoughts. In arriving at your assessment consider the basis for, and proven effectiveness of, the approaches that have been deployed.

Perceived strengths (+)	Perceived areas for improvement (-)

Note: List also as areas for improvement relevant activities that you feel should be initiated and are not at present undertaken.

This criterion involves an assessment of the organization's mission, values, vision and strategic direction and the ways in which it achieves them.

Policy and Strategy 2e

2e How policy and strategies are regularly reviewed and improved

Areas to address could include:

How the organization evaluates the relevance and effectiveness of its policy and strategy.

How the frequency of the reviews is determined and how appropriate changes are made.

Step 1. Assess importance of criterion

	These are not key issues	These issues are moderately important	These issues are important	These issues are critical
Importance Rating	(0)	(1)	(2)	(3)

Note: Tick a box to indicate your view of the importance of this criterion (note, the description of the criterion is the words after 2e)

Step 2. Detail your overall process

Note: List the overall process you use to manage all the activities related to this criterion

Step 3. List specific policies, processes and practices

Step 4. For each activity listed in step 3 list how long you have been using each policy, process or practice (years/months)

Step 5. List to what extent you want to deploy each policy, process and practice and how far they have been deployed to date (e.g. by site, organizational level, department, activity, product etc.)

Step 6. List how and how often you review the effectiveness of each activity and the overall process.

Note: Annotate your comments onto the list from Step 3

Step 7. List improvements resulting from reviews

Step 8. Review your comments on steps 1 to 7 as a whole, and form and record an opinion on the success of the approaches used and their deployment. List this as a set of composite perceived strengths and areas for improvement. The scoring card in Appendix 3 should be used to help your thoughts. In arriving at your assessment consider the basis for, and proven effectiveness of, the approaches that have been deployed.

Perceived strengths (+)	Perceived areas for improvement (-)

Note: List also as areas for improvement relevant activities that you feel should be initiated and are not at present undertaken.

You have now completed Criterion 2 - Note any actions required.

Criterion 3 - People Management

This criterion looks at how your organization releases the full potential of its people. The next 10 pages will help you caputre your views on 3a to 3e.

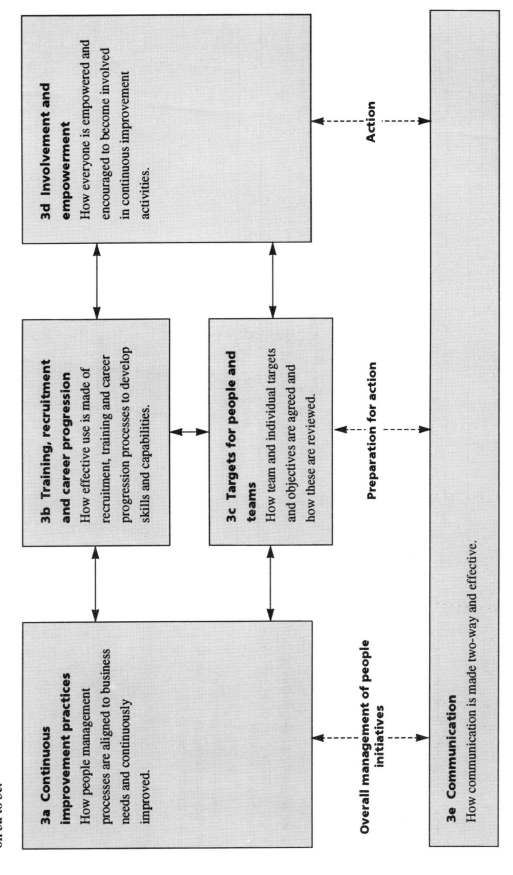

3a Continuous improvement practices
How people management processes are aligned to business needs and continuously improved.

3b Training, recruitment and career progression
How effective use is made of recruitment, training and career progression processes to develop skills and capabilities.

3c Targets for people and teams
How team and individual targets and objectives are agreed and how these are reviewed.

3d Involvement and empowerment
How everyone is empowered and encouraged to become involved in continuous improvement activities.

3e Communication
How communication is made two-way and effective.

Overall management of people initiatives

Preparation for action

Action

This criterion involves an assessment of the management of the organization's people and how it releases their full potential to improve its business continuously.

People Management 3a

3a How continuous improvement in people management is accomplished

Areas to address could include:

How people management plans are aligned to organizational policy and strategy.

How the success of the organization's people management policies are reviewed and how they are improved.

How appropriate direct and indirect employee satisfaction data is monitored and used (see also criterion 7).

Step 1. Assess importance of criterion

	These are not key issues	These issues are moderately important	These issues are important	These issues are critical
	(0)	(1)	(2)	(3)
Importance Rating				

Note: Tick a box to indicate your view of the importance of this criterion (note, the description of the criterion is the words after 3a)

Step 2. Detail your overall process

Note: List the overall process you use to manage all the activities related to this criterion

Step 3. List specific policies, processes and practices

Step 4. For each activity listed in step 3 list how long you have been using each policy, process or practice (years/months)

Step 5. List to what extent you want to deploy each policy, process and practice and how far they have been deployed to date (e.g. by site, organizational level, department, activity, product etc.)

Step 6. List how and how often you review the effectiveness of each activity and the overall process.

Note: Annotate your comments onto the list from Step 3

Step 7. List improvements resulting from reviews

Step 8. Review your comments on steps 1 to 7 as a whole, and form and record an opinion on the success of the approaches used and their deployment. List this as a set of composite perceived strengths and areas for improvement. The scoring card in Appendix 3 should be used to help your thoughts. In arriving at your assessment consider the basis for, and proven effectiveness of, the approaches that have been deployed.

Perceived strengths (+)	Perceived areas for improvement (-)

Note: List also as areas for improvement relevant activities that you feel should be initiated and are not at present undertaken.

This criterion involves an assessment of the management of the organization's people and how it releases their full potential to improve its business continuously.

People Management 3b

3b How skills and capabilities are preserved and developed through recruitment, training and career progression

Areas to address could include:

How skills profiles are obtained, used and aligned to organizational requirements.

How training, development and manpower planning is undertaken and implemented.

How the effectiveness of training is measured.

How recruitment, career and succession planning is undertaken.

How people are developed through team work and how individual skills are improved through working in teams.

Step 1. Assess importance of criterion

	These are not key issues	These issues are moderately important	These issues are important	These issues are critical
Importance Rating	(0)	(1)	(2)	(3)

Note: Tick a box to indicate your view of the importance of this criterion (note, the description of the criterion is the words after 3b)

Step 2. Detail your overall process

Note: List the overall process you use to manage all the activities related to this criterion

Step 3. List specific policies, processes and practices

Step 4. For each activity listed in step 3 list how long you have been using each policy, process or practice (years/months)

Step 5. List to what extent you want to deploy each policy, process and practice and how far they have been deployed to date (e.g. by site, organizational level, department, activity, product etc.)

Step 6. List how and how often you review the effectiveness of each activity and the overall process.

Note: Annotate your comments onto the list from Step 3

Step 7. List improvements resulting from reviews

Step 8. Review your comments on steps 1 to 7 as a whole, and form and record an opinion on the success of the approaches used and their deployment. List this as a set of composite perceived strengths and areas for improvement. The scoring card in Appendix 3 should be used to help your thoughts. In arriving at your assessment consider the basis for, and proven effectiveness of, the approaches that have been deployed.

Perceived strengths (+)

Perceived areas for improvement (-)

Note: List also as areas for improvement relevant activities that you feel should be initiated and are not at present undertaken.

This criterion involves an assessment of the management of the organization's people and how it releases their full potential to improve its business continuously.

People Management 3c

3c How people and teams agree targets and continuously review performance

Areas to address could include:

How personal and team objectives are agreed.

How personal and team objectives are aligned with organizational targets.

How individual and team objectives are reviewed and updated.

How people are appraised in their performance to targets or objectives and how help and assistance is provided.

Step 1. Assess importance of criterion

	These are not key issues	These issues are moderately important	These issues are important	These issues are critical
	(0)	(1)	(2)	(3)
Importance Rating				

Note: Tick a box to indicate your view of the importance of this criterion (note, the description of the criterion is the words after 3c)

Step 2. Detail your overall process

Note: List the overall process you use to manage all the activities related to this criterion

Step 3. List specific policies, processes and practices

Step 4. For each activity listed in step 3 list how long you have been using each policy, process or practice (years/months)

Step 5. List to what extent you want to deploy each policy, process and practice and how far they have been deployed to date (e.g. by site, organizational level, department, activity, product etc.)

Step 6. List how and how often you review the effectiveness of each activity and the overall process.

Note: Annotate your comments onto the list from Step 3

Step 7. List improvements resulting from reviews

Step 8. Review your comments on steps 1 to 7 as a whole, and form and record an opinion on the success of the approaches used and their deployment. List this as a set of composite perceived strengths and areas for improvement. The scoring card in Appendix 3 should be used to help your thoughts. In arriving at your assessment consider the basis for, and proven effectiveness of, the approaches that have been deployed.

Perceived strengths (+)

Perceived areas for improvement (-)

Note: List also as areas for improvement relevant activities that you feel should be initiated and are not at present undertaken.

People Management 3d

This criterion involves an assessment of the management of the organization's people and how it releases their full potential to improve its business continuously.

3d How involvement of all in continuous improvement is promoted and how employees are empowered to take appropriate action

Areas to address could include:

How the organization's people are empowered and how the effectiveness of the empowerment is measured.

How appropriate involvement and improvement contributions are encouraged from individuals and teams.

How the effectiveness of improvement contributions is measured.

How events such as in-house conferences and seminars are used to encourage peoples further involvement in continuous improvement.

Step 1. Assess importance of criterion

	These are not key issues	These issues are moderately important	These issues are important	These issues are critical
Importance Rating	(0)	(1)	(2)	(3)

Note: Tick a box to indicate your view of the importance of this criterion (note, the description of the criterion is the words after 3d)

Step 2. Detail your overall process

Note: List the overall process you use to manage all the activities related to this criterion

Step 3. List specific policies, processes and practices

Step 4. For each activity listed in step 3 list how long you have been using each policy, process or practice (years/months)

Step 5. List to what extent you want to deploy each policy, process and practice and how far they have been deployed to date (e.g. by site, organizational level, department, activity, product etc.)

Step 6. List how and how often you review the effectiveness of each activity and the overall process.

Note: Annotate your comments onto the list from Step 3

Step 7. List improvements resulting from reviews

Step 8. Review your comments on steps 1 to 7 as a whole, and form and record an opinion on the success of the approaches used and their deployment. List this as a set of composite perceived strengths and areas for improvement. The scoring card in Appendix 3 should be used to help your thoughts. In arriving at your assessment consider the basis for, and proven effectiveness of, the approaches that have been deployed.

Perceived strengths (+)

Perceived areas for improvement (-)

Note: List also as areas for improvement relevant activities that you feel should be initiated and are not at present undertaken.

This criterion involves an assessment of the management of the organization's people and how it releases their full potential to improve its business continuously.

People Management 3e

3e How effective top-down, bottom-up communication is achieved

Areas to address could include:

How the general communication needs of managers, employees and other relevant audiences are identified.

How appropriate media are selected and used to transmit information to the organization's people.

How two way communication is assured.

How the effectiveness of communication is measured, reviewed and improved.

How the organization openly receives information and views from its people.

Step 1. Assess importance of criterion

	These are not key issues	These issues are moderately important	These issues are important	These issues are critical
	(0)	(1)	(2)	(3)
Importance Rating				

Note: Tick a box to indicate your view of the importance of this criterion (note, the description of the criterion is the words after 3e)

Step 2. Detail your overall process

Note: List the overall process you use to manage all the activities related to this criterion

Step 3. List specific policies, processes and practices

Step 4. For each activity listed in step 3 list how long you have been using each policy, process or practice (years/months)

Step 5. List to what extent you want to deploy each policy, process and practice and how far they have been deployed to date (e.g. by site, organizational level, department, activity, product etc.)

Step 6. List how and how often you review the effectiveness of each activity and the overall process.

Note: Annotate your comments onto the list from Step 3

Step 7. List improvements resulting from reviews

Step 8. Review your comments on steps 1 to 7 as a whole, and form and record an opinion on the success of the approaches used and their deployment. List this as a set of composite perceived strengths and areas for improvement. The scoring card in Appendix 3 should be used to help your thoughts. In arriving at your assessment consider the basis for, and proven effectiveness of, the approaches that have been deployed.

Perceived strengths (+)

Perceived areas for improvement (-)

Note: List also as areas for improvement relevant activities that you feel should be initiated and are not at present undertaken.

You have now completed Criterion 3 - Note any actions required.

Criterion 4 - Resources

This criterion looks at the ways your organization manages its key resources in support of its policy and strategy. The next 8 pages will help you capture your views on 4a to 4d.

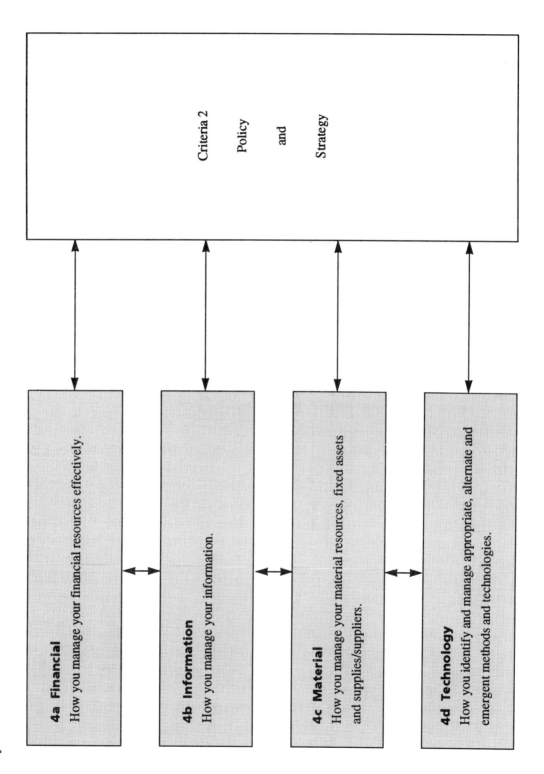

This criterion involves an assessment of how the organization improves, manages, uses and preserves its resources and the effectiveness by which they are deployed in support of its policy and strategy.

4a How financial resources are managed, utilized and preserved

Areas to address could include:

How financial strategies and processes reflect and support quality and continuous improvement principles and values.

How financial management practices are aligned to user needs.

How financial strategies and practices are reviewed and improved.

How key financial parameters (e.g. cash flow, balance sheet elements, share holder value etc.) are managed for improvement.

How new activities/ideas that require investment are evaluated.

How the underlying processes of financial management are aligned to the organization's overall strategies.

Resources 4a

Step 2. Detail your overall process

Note: List the overall process you use to manage all the activities related to this criterion

Step 1. Assess importance of criterion

	These are not key issues	These issues are moderately important	These issues are important	These issues are critical
Importance Rating	(0)	(1)	(2)	(3)

Note: Tick a box to indicate your view of the importance of this criterion (note, the description of the criterion is the words after 4a)

Step 3. List specific policies, processes and practices

Step 4. For each activity listed in step 3 list how long you have been using each policy, process or practice (years/months)

Step 5. List to what extent you want to deploy each policy, process and practice and how far they have been deployed to date (e.g. by site, organizational level, department, activity, product etc.)

Step 6. List how and how often you review the effectiveness of each activity and the overall process.

Note: Annotate your comments onto the list from Step 3

Step 7. List improvements resulting from reviews

Step 8. Review your comments on steps 1 to 7 as a whole, and form and record an opinion on the success of the approaches used and their deployment. List this as a set of composite perceived strengths and areas for improvement. The scoring card in Appendix 3 should be used to help your thoughts. In arriving at your assessment consider the basis for, and proven effectiveness of, the approaches that have been deployed.

Perceived strengths (+)

Perceived areas for improvement (-)

Note: List also as areas for improvement relevant activities that you feel should be initiated and are not at present undertaken.

This criterion involves an assessment of how the organization improves, manages, uses and preserves its resources and the effectiveness by which they are deployed in support of its policy and strategy.

Resources 4b

4b How information resources are managed, utilized and preserved

Areas to address could include:

How information systems are managed and reflect user needs.

How information validity, integrity, security and scope are assured and improved.

How information is made accessible to those who need it and how this is determined e.g. customers, suppliers and people in the organization.

How information strategies support the principles of quality and continuous improvement for example by collection of data on improvement and/or competitors.

How the underlying processes of information management are aligned to the organization and overall strategies.

Step 1. Assess importance of criterion

	These are not key issues	These issues are moderately important	These issues are important	These issues are critical
Importance Rating	(0)	(1)	(2)	(3)

Note: Tick a box to indicate your view of the importance of this criterion (note, the description of the criterion is the words after 4b)

Step 2. Detail your overall process

Note: List the overall process you use to manage all the activities related to this criterion

Step 3. List specific policies, processes and practices

Step 4. For each activity listed in step 3 list how long you have been using each policy, process or practice (years/months)

Step 5. List to what extent you want to deploy each policy, process and practice and how far they have been deployed to date (e.g. by site, organizational level, department, activity, product etc.)

Step 6. List how and how often you review the effectiveness of each activity and the overall process.

Note: Annotate your comments onto the list from Step 3

Step 7. List improvements resulting from reviews

Step 8. Review your comments on steps 1 to 7 as a whole, and form and record an opinion on the success of the approaches used and their deployment. List this as a set of composite perceived strengths and areas for improvement. The scoring card in Appendix 3 should be used to help your thoughts. In arriving at your assessment consider the basis for, and proven effectiveness of, the approaches that have been deployed.

Perceived strengths (+)

Perceived areas for improvement (−)

Note: List also as areas for improvement relevant activities that you feel should be initiated and are not at present undertaken.

This criterion involves an assessment of how the organization improves, manages, uses and preserves its resources and the effectiveness by which they are deployed in support of its policy and strategy.

Resources 4c

4c How material resources are managed, utilized and preserved

Areas to address could include:

How suppliers are managed and procurement strategies set.

How material inventories are optimised e.g. through JIT, stock control, waste management, or other practices.

How utilization of fixed assets is optimized and how they are protected.

How waste is minimized.

How the underlying processes of material management are aligned to the organization and its overall strategies.

Step 1. Assess importance of criterion

	These are not key issues	These issues are moderately important	These issues are important	These issues are critical
Importance Rating	(0)	(1)	(2)	(3)

Note: Tick a box to indicate your view of the importance of this criterion (note, the description of the criterion is the words after 4c)

Step 2. Detail your overall process

Note: List the overall process you use to manage all the activities related to this criterion

Step 3. List specific policies, processes and practices

Step 4. For each activity listed in step 3 list how long you have been using each policy, process or practice (years/months)

Step 5. List to what extent you want to deploy each policy, process and practice and how far they have been deployed to date (e.g. by site, organizational level, department, activity, product etc.)

Step 6. List how and how often you review the effectiveness of each activity and the overall process.

Note: Annotate your comments onto the list from Step 3

Step 7. List improvements resulting from reviews

Step 8. Review your comments on steps 1 to 7 as a whole, and form and record an opinion on the success of the approaches used and their deployment. List this as a set of composite perceived strengths and areas for improvement. The scoring card in Appendix 3 should be used to help your thoughts. In arriving at your assessment consider the basis for, and proven effectiveness of, the approaches that have been deployed.

Perceived strengths (+)

Perceived areas for improvement (-)

Note: List also as areas for improvement relevant activities that you feel should be initiated and are not at present undertaken.

This criterion involves an assessment of how the organization improves, manages, uses and preserves its resources and the effectiveness by which they are deployed in support of its policy and strategy.

Resources 4d

4d How technology resources are managed, utilized and preserved

Areas to address could include:

How machines, processes, ideas etc, related to alternative and emerging technologies are identified and evaluated.

How technology has been exploited to secure competitive advantage.

How the development of people skills and capabilities is harmonized with the development of technology.

How technology is harnessed in support of improvement in processes, information systems and other systems.

How intellectual property is protected and exploited.

How the underlying processes of technology management are aligned to the organization and overall strategies.

Step 1. Assess importance of criterion

	These are not key issues	These issues are moderately important	These issues are important	These issues are critical
Importance Rating	(0)	(1)	(2)	(3)

Note: Tick a box to indicate your view of the importance of this criterion (note, the description of the criterion is the words after 4d)

Step 2. Detail your overall process

Note: List the overall process you use to manage all the activities related to this criterion

Step 3. List specific policies, processes and practices

Step 4. For each activity listed in step 3 list how long you have been using each policy, process or practice (years/months)

Step 5. List to what extent you want to deploy each policy, process and practice and how far they have been deployed to date (e.g. by site, organizational level, department, activity, product etc.)

Step 6. List how and how often you review the effectiveness of each activity and the overall process.

Note: Annotate your comments onto the list from Step 3

Step 7. List improvements resulting from reviews

Step 8. Review your comments on steps 1 to 7 as a whole, and form and record an opinion on the success of the approaches used and their deployment. List this as a set of composite perceived strengths and areas for improvement. The scoring card in Appendix 3 should be used to help your thoughts. In arriving at your assessment consider the basis for, and proven effectiveness of, the approaches that have been deployed.

Perceived strengths (+)

Perceived areas for improvement (-)

Note: List also as areas for improvement relevant activities that you feel should be initiated and are not at present undertaken.

You have now completed **Criterion 4** - Note any actions required.

Criterion 5 - Processes

This criterion looks at how you identify, manage, review and where appropriate, revise your organization's processes. The next 10 pages will help you capture your views on 5a to 5e.

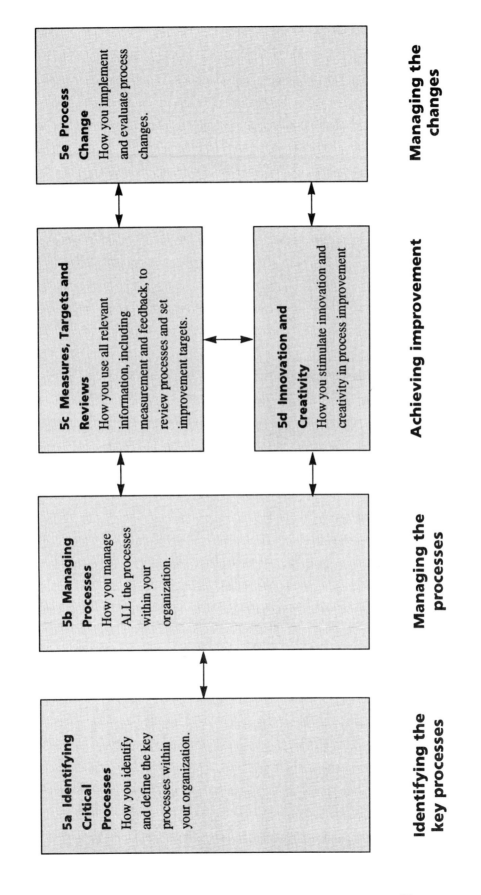

5a Identifying Critical Processes
How you identify and define the key processes within your organization.

Identifying the key processes

5b Managing Processes
How you manage ALL the processes within your organization.

Managing the processes

5c Measures, Targets and Reviews
How you use all relevant information, including measurement and feedback, to review processes and set improvement targets.

5d Innovation and Creativity
How you stimulate innovation and creativity in process improvement

Achieving improvement

5e Process Change
How you implement and evaluate process changes.

Managing the changes

This criterion involves an assessment of the organization's approach to the management of its value adding activities.

Processes 5a

5a How processes critical to the success of the organization are identified

Areas to address could include:

How the critical processes are identified.

How critical processes are defined and what they currently are.

How interface issues are resolved.

How impact on the business is evaluated.

How future stakeholder needs are predicted and incorporated into the process of identification of critical processes.

Note: critical processes will normally have an output which is a result which may be presented in criteria 6, 7, 8 or 9.

For example invoicing and collection of debt may well be determined as key or critical processes, the output or success of which would be reported in Criterion 9.

Further examples of key or critical processes could include provision of raw materials and supplies, manufacturing, related processes, engineering related processes, reception of orders, delivery of product or service, determination of customer and people satisfaction, design, new product and service development, marketing, budgeting and planning, and management of safety, health and

Step 1. Assess importance of criterion

	These are not key issues	These issues are moderately important	These issues are important	These issues are critical
Importance Rating	(0)	(1)	(2)	(3)

Note: Tick a box to indicate your view of the importance of this criterion (note, the description of the criterion is the words after 5a)

Step 2. Detail your overall process

Note: List the overall process you use to manage all the activities related to this criterion

Step 3. List specific policies, processes and practices

Step 4. For each activity listed in step 3 list how long you have been using each policy, process or practice (years/months)

Step 5. List to what extent you want to deploy each policy, process and practice and how far they have been deployed to date (e.g. by site, organizational level, department, activity, product etc.)

Step 6. List how and how often you review the effectiveness of each activity and the overall process.

Note: Annotate your comments onto the list from Step 3

Step 7. List improvements resulting from reviews

Step 8. Review your comments on steps 1 to 7 as a whole, and form and record an opinion on the success of the approaches used and their deployment. List this as a set of composite perceived strengths and areas for improvement. The scoring card in Appendix 3 should be used to help your thoughts. In arriving at your assessment consider the basis for, and proven effectiveness of, the approaches that have been deployed.

Perceived strengths (+)

Perceived areas for improvement (-)

Note: List also as areas for improvement relevant activities that you feel should be initiated and are not at present undertaken.

This criterion involves an assessment of the organization's approach to the management of its value adding activities.

Processes 5b

5b How the organization systematically manages its processes

Areas to address could include:

How process ownership is determined.

How standards of operation are established and monitored and by whom.

How performance measures are used in process management.

The possible relevance of quality system standards, such as the ISO 9000 series and how they are applied.

Step 1. Assess importance of criterion

	These are not key issues	These issues are moderately important	These issues are important	These issues are critical
		(0)	(1)	(2)	(3)
Importance Rating				

Note: Tick a box to indicate your view of the importance of this criterion (note, the description of the criterion is the words after 5b)

Step 2. Detail your overall process

Note: List the overall process you use to manage all the activities related to this criterion

Step 3. List specific policies, processes and practices

Step 4. For each activity listed in step 3 list how long you have been using each policy, process or practice (years/months)

Step 5. List to what extent you want to deploy each policy, process and practice and how far they have been deployed to date (e.g. by site, organizational level, department, activity, product etc.)

Step 6. List how and how often you review the effectiveness of each activity and the overall process.

Note: Annotate your comments onto the list from Step 3

Step 7. List improvements resulting from reviews

Step 8. Review your comments on steps 1 to 7 as a whole, and form and record an opinion on the success of the approaches used and their deployment. List this as a set of composite perceived strengths and areas for improvement. The scoring card in Appendix 3 should be used to help your thoughts. In arriving at your assessment consider the basis for, and proven effectiveness of, the approaches that have been deployed.

Perceived strengths (+)	Perceived areas for improvement (-)

Note: List also as areas for improvement relevant activities that you feel should be initiated and are not at present undertaken.

Processes 5c

This criterion involves an assessment of the organization's approach to the management of its value adding activities.

5c How process performance measures along with all relevant feedback are used to review processes and set improvement targets

Areas to address could include:

How information from employees, customers, suppliers and competitors is used in target setting.

How 'benchmark' or standard data is used in target setting.

How current performance measurement and improvement targets are related to past achievement.

How the processes critical to the success of the business are reviewed.

How challenging improvement targets are set, aligned to business goals and agreed.

Step 1. Assess importance of criterion

	These are not key issues	These issues are moderately important	These issues are important	These issues are critical
Importance Rating	(0)	(1)	(2)	(3)

Note: Tick a box to indicate your view of the importance of this criterion (note, the description of the criterion is the words after 5c)

Step 2. Detail your overall process

Note: List the overall process you use to manage all the activities related to this criterion

Step 3. List specific policies, processes and practices

Step 4. For each activity listed in step 3 list how long you have been using each policy, process or practice (years/months)

Step 5. List to what extent you want to deploy each policy, process and practice and how far they have been deployed to date (e.g. by site, organizational level, department, activity, product etc.)

Step 6. List how and how often you review the effectiveness of each activity and the overall process.

Note: Annotate your comments onto the list from Step 3

Step 7. List improvements resulting from reviews

Step 8. Review your comments on steps 1 to 7 as a whole, and form and record an opinion on the success of the approaches used and their deployment. List this as a set of composite perceived strengths and areas for improvement. The scoring card in Appendix 3 should be used to help your thoughts. In arriving at your assessment consider the basis for, and proven effectiveness of, the approaches that have been deployed.

Perceived strengths (+)

Perceived areas for improvement (-)

Note: List also as areas for improvement relevant activities that you feel should be initiated and are not at present undertaken.

This criterion involves an assessment of the organization's approach to the management of its value adding activities.

Processes 5d

5d How the organization stimulates innovation and creativity in process improvement

Areas to address could include:

How new principles of design, new technology and new operating philosophies are identified, appraised and where appropriate introduced.

How employees are encouraged to make innovative and creative inputs to process improvement.

How organizational structures have been changed to encourage innovation and creativity.

Step 1. Assess importance of criterion

	These are not key issues	These issues are moderately important	These issues are important	These issues are critical
Importance Rating	(0)	(1)	(2)	(3)

Note: Tick a box to indicate your view of the importance of this criterion (note, the description of the criterion is the words after 5d)

Step 2. Detail your overall process

Note: List the overall process you use to manage all the activities related to this criterion

Step 3. List specific policies, processes and practices

Step 4. For each activity listed in step 3 list how long you have been using each policy, process or practice (years/months)

Step 5. List to what extent you want to deploy each policy, process and practice and how far they have been deployed to date (e.g. by site, organizational level, department, activity, product etc.)

Step 6. List how and how often you review the effectiveness of each activity and the overall process.

Note: Annotate your comments onto the list from Step 3

Step 7. List improvements resulting from reviews

Step 8. Review your comments on steps 1 to 7 as a whole, and form and record an opinion on the success of the approaches used and and their deployment. List this as a set of composite perceived strengths and areas for improvement. The scoring card in Appendix 3 should be used to help your thoughts. In arriving at your assessment consider the basis for, and proven effectiveness of, the approaches that have been deployed.

Perceived strengths (+)

Perceived areas for improvement (-)

Note: List also as areas for improvement relevant activities that you feel should be initiated and are not at present undertaken.

This criterion involves an assessment of the organization's approach to the management of its value adding activities.

Processes 5e

5e How the organization implements changes and evaluation of benefits

Areas to address could include:

How new or changed processes are piloted and implementation controlled.

How process changes are communicated.

How staff are trained prior to implementation of changes.

How process changes are reviewed to ensure that the predicted results are obtained.

Step 1. Assess importance of criterion

	These are not key issues	These issues are moderately important	These issues are important	These issues are critical
Importance Rating	(0)	(1)	(2)	(3)

Note: Tick a box to indicate your view of the importance of this criterion (note, the description of the criterion is the words after 5e)

Step 2. Detail your overall process

Note: List the overall process you use to manage all the activities related to this criterion

Step 3. List specific policies, processes and practices

Step 4. For each activity listed in step 3 list how long you have been using each policy, process or practice (years/months)

Step 5. List to what extent you want to deploy each policy, process and practice and how far they have been deployed to date (e.g. by site, organizational level, department, activity, product etc.)

Step 6. List how and how often you review the effectiveness of each activity and the overall process.

Note: Annotate your comments onto the list from Step 3

Step 7. List improvements resulting from reviews

Step 8. Review your comments on steps 1 to 7 as a whole, and form and record an opinion on the success of the approaches used and their deployment. List this as a set of composite perceived strengths and areas for improvement. The scoring card in Appendix 3 should be used to help your thoughts. In arriving at your assessment consider the basis for, and proven effectiveness of, the approaches that have been deployed.

Perceived strengths (+)	Perceived areas for improvement (-)

Note: List also as areas for improvement relevant activities that you feel should be initiated and are not at present undertaken.

You have now completed Criterion 5 - Note any actions required.

Criterion 6 - Customer Satisfaction Results

Direct Results		Indirect Results
Perception measures and results i.e. judgement by the customers	**+**	Predicting, leading and influencing measures and results i.e. judgement by the organization

Assessed by:

a. The organizations actual performance.

b. The organizations own targets.

c. Comparison with the performance of competitors.

d. Comparison with the performance of 'best in class' organizations.

e. The 'proven' relevance/priority, to the customer, of the measures put forward.

f. The breadth and the scope of the measures.

This criterion involves assessing and predicting the external customers' perceptions regarding the organization

Customer Satisfaction 6

Results to report could include:

6.1 Direct customer perception measures of the product/service/organization:

Specific attributes to survey could include:

- capability meeting of specifications - defect error or rejection rates - consistency reproducability - maintainability - durability - reliability - on time delivery - in full delivery - logistic information - delivery frequency - responsiveness and flexibility - product availability - accessibility of key staff - product training - product literature - sales support - technical support - simplicity, convenience and accuracy of documentation - awareness of customer problems - complaint handling - warranty and guarantee provisions - spare part availability - innovation and service quality - product development - payment terms and financing.

6.2 Indirect measures or predictors of customer satisfaction which could inlcude:

- complaint levels - praise logs
- letters of thanks - customers queries/errors/ returns
- reworks - non-conformances that directly impacts customer service
- repeat business measures
- levels of lost or new business
- levels of compensation or warranty claims
- market share
- media articles/accolades/awards received.

Step 1. Assess importance of criterion

	These are not key issues	These issues are moderately important	These issues are important	These issues are critical
Importance Rating	(0)	(1)	(2)	(3)

Note: Tick a box to indicate your view of the importance of this criterion (note, the description of the criterion is the words after 6.1 or 6.2)

Step 2. Describe the overall process

Note: List the process by which you decide with your customers what is relevant data to collect, how targets for performance are set, and how the data is gathered.

Step 3. List the specific direct and indirect data that you use to assess customer satisfaction

Step 4. Note which data recorded in step 3 is showing positive or negative trends and for how long.
Step 5. Note which data is meeting or exceeding the targets you set.

Note: Annotate your notes onto the list from step 3

Step 6. Assess the relationship of your results with competitors and or best in class organizations and list your key successes.

Note: Annotate your notes onto the list from step 3

Step 7. List any results, that you perceive to be relevant to your customers, that are not covered by the data you collect.

Step 8. Form and record an opinion on the scope, trends, levels and comparisons of your performance. List this as perceived strengths and areas for improvement. The scoring 'card' in Appendix 3 may help in the process.

Perceived strengths (+)	Perceived areas for improvement (-)

Note: List any relevant measures or comparisons that you feel should be initiated, and are not at present, as areas for improvement.

You have now completed Criterion 6 - Note any actions required.

Criterion 7 - People Satisfaction Results

Assessed by:

a. The organizations actual performance.

b. The organizations own targets.

c. Comparison with the performance of competitors.

d. Comparison with the performance of 'best in class' organizations.

e. The 'proven' relevance/priority, to the employees, of the measures put forward.

f. The breadth and the scope of the measures.

Direct Results

Perception measures and results i.e. judgement by the people/employees

+

Indirect Results

Predicting, leading and influencing measures and results i.e. judgement by the organization

This criterion involves assessing employees feelings about the organization

People Satisfaction 7

Step 1. Assess importance of criterion

	These are not key issues	These issues are moderately important	These issues are important	These issues are critical
Importance Rating	(0)	(1)	(2)	(3)

Note: Tick a box to indicate your view of the importance of this criterion (note, the description of the criterion is the words after 7.1 or 7.2)

Step 2. Describe the overall process

Note: List the process by which you decide with your employees what is relevant data to collect, how targets for performance are set, and how the data is gathered.

Step 3. List the specific direct and indirect data that you use to assess people satisfaction

Results to report could include:

7.1 Direct measure of employees feelings/satisfaction including data from:

- employee satisfaction surveys upward assessments - feedback on training courses - feedback on conferences - staff forums - staff AGMs - inputs into behavioural measurement of managers etc.

Specific areas to address in such surveys/feedback systems could inlcude:

- working environment/location/space/ amenities - health and safety provisions - communications at local and organizational level - career prospects and planning - appraisal and targets setting - training development and retraining - awareness of the requirements of job - awareness of the organization's values, vision and strategy - awareness of total quality processes - involvement in total quality processes - recognition schemes - reward schemes - organizational management - management style - job security.

7.2 Indirect predictors of employee satisfaction could include:

- staff turnover - grievances - levels of staff suggestion - sickness - lateness - disciplinary trends - recruitment trends - improvement ideas - use of company provided facilities.

Step 4. Note which data recorded in step 3 is showing positive or negative trends and for how long.

Step 5. Note which data is meeting or exceeding the targets you set.

Note: Annotate your notes onto the list from step 3

Step 6. Assess the relationship of your results with competitors and or best in class organizations and list your key successes.

Note: Annotate your notes onto the list from step 3

Step 7. List any results, that you perceive to be relevant to your employees, that are not covered by the data you collect.

Step 8. Form and record an opinion on the scope, trends, levels and comparisons of your performance. List this as perceived strengths and areas for improvement. The scoring 'card' in Appendix 3 may help in the process.

Perceived strengths (+)	Perceived areas for improvement (-)

Note: List any relevant measures or comparisons that you feel should be initiated, and are not at present, as areas for improvement.

You have now completed Criterion 7 - Note any actions required.

Criterion 8 – Impact on Society Results

Assessed by:

a. The organizations actual performance.

b. The organizations own targets.

c. Comparison with the performance of competitors.

d. Comparison with the performance of 'best in class' organizations.

e. The 'proven' relevance/priority, to 'society', of the measures put forward.

f. The breadth and the scope of the measures.

50%	**Direct Results** Perception measures and results i.e. judgement by the community at large
	+
50%	**Indirect Results** Predicting, leading and influencing measures and results i.e. judgement by the organization

Impact on Society 8

This criterion involves assessing and predicting the perception of the organization among the community at large. This includes views on the organizations approach to the quality of life, the environment and to the preservation of global resources.

Results to report could include:

8.1 Wherever possible perceptions of the local and wider community with respect to the organization's performance should be given.

8.2 Where this is not possible indirect data should be disclosed reflecting:

- trends of active involvement in community support such as charity support, participation in community events, involvement in education and training, volunteering, environmental and ecological improvement activity, medical welfare activities and sports and leisure activities.

- trends in activities to reduce and prevent nuisance and harm to neighbours as a result of operations, business related transportation and products e.g. noise and pollution reduction activities, vehicle access, hazards and health risk managment.

- trends and activities to assist the preservation of global resources such as energy, material resources, conservation, use of recycled material, reduction of waste, recycling, environmental and ecological impact issues.

- trends and levels in related predictors such as general complaints, statutory infringements, accolades, awards received, media coverage, number of safety related incidents, impact on the employment level of the local community and infringements of relevant standards or regulations.

Step 1. Assess importance of criterion

	These are not key issues	These issues are moderately important	These issues are important	These issues are critical
	(0)	(1)	(2)	(3)
Importance Rating				

Note: Tick a box to indicate your view of the importance of this criterion (note, the description of the criterion is the words after 8.1 or 8.2)

Step 2. Describe the overall process

Note: List the process by which you decide what is relevant data to collect, how targets for performance are set, and how the data is gathered.

Step 3. List the specific direct and indirect data that you use to assess 'Impact on Society'

Step 4. Note which data recorded in step 3 is showing positive or negative trends and for how long.

Step 5. Note which data is meeting or exceeding the targets you set.

Note: Annotate your notes onto the list from step 3

Step 6. Assess the relationship of your results with competitors and or best in class organizations and list your key successes.

Note: Annotate your notes onto the list from step 3

Step 7. List any results, that you perceive to be relevant, that are not covered by the data you collect.

Step 8. Form and record an opinion on the scope, trends, levels and comparisons of your performance. List this as perceived strengths and areas for improvement. The scoring 'card' in Appendix 3 may help in the process.

Perceived strengths (+)	Perceived areas for improvement (-)

Note: List any relevant measures or comparisons that you feel should be initiated, and are not at present, as areas for improvement.

You have now completed **Criterion 8** - Note any actions required.

Criterion 9 - Business Results

Assessed by:

a. The organizations actual performance.

b. The organizations own targets.

c. Comparison with the performance of competitors.

d. Comparison with the performance of 'best in class' organizations.

e. The 'proven' relevance/priority, to the 'stakeholders', of the measures put forward.

f. The breadth and the scope of the measures.

Direct Results

Financial, 'Bottom Line' results.

+

Indirect Results

Key efficiency and effectiveness measures and the results of the key processes identified in criteria 4 and 5.

Business Results 9

This criterion involves an assessment of what the organization is achieving in relation to its planned business performance.

Results to report could include:

9.1 Direct financial measures including:

Budgetary performance/profit
Revenue and cost ratios
Cash flow
Sales
Value added analysis
Losses
Shareholder returns and value
Liquidity and working capital

9.2 Indirect non-financial data could include:

These should relate to the achievement of key business targets/objectives and will typically include:

Vital internal efficiency/effectiveness measures
Trends and comparisons on the outputs of key processes
Key quality measures
Market share analysis
Waste trends
Key production or service volumes
Cycle time reduction on key activities and targets e.g. order processing, delivery, time to bring new products to market
Inventory turnover etc.

Step 1. Assess importance of criterion

	These are not key issues	These issues are moderately important	These issues are important	These issues are critical
Importance Rating	(0)	(1)	(2)	(3)

Note: Tick a box to indicate your view of the importance of this criterion (note, the description of the criterion is the words after 9.1 or 9.2)

Step 2. Describe the overall process

Note: List the process by which you decide with your stakeholders what is relevant data to collect, how targets for performance are set, and how the data is gathered.

Step 3. List the specific direct and indirect data that you use to assess business results

Step 4. Note which data recorded in step 3 is showing positive or negative trends and for how long.

Step 5. Note which data is meeting or exceeding the targets you set.

Note: Annotate your notes onto the list from step 3

Step 6. Assess the relationship of your results with competitors and or best in class organizations and list your key successes.

Note: Annotate your notes onto the list from step 3

Step 7. List any results, that you perceive to be relevant, that are not covered by the data you collect.

Step 8. Form and record an opinion on the scope, trends, levels and comparisons of your performance. List this as perceived strengths and areas for improvement. The scoring 'card' in Appendix 3 may help in the process.

Perceived strengths (+)

Perceived areas for improvement (-)

Note: List any relevant measures or comparisons that you feel should be initiated, and are not at present, as areas for improvement.

You have now completed **Criterion 9** - Note any actions required.

Appendix 1

Relative strengths of different self assessment methods

The table below shows a recent analysis produced by Bristol Quality Centre for the EFQM of some different methods of self assessment and their relative strengths. Each is described below in more detail.

Organizations typically 'mature' from an initial process such as a workshop to more detailed methods of data collection. The steps outlined previously in section 5.2 maybe useful to help analyse and plan the adoption of a particular method.

	Effort	Ability to use output for Action Planning	Analysis of perceived strengths/areas for improvement	Accuracy of score
1 Producing an award style self application report (75 page written document)	High	Good	Detailed	High
2 Facilitator led workshop assessments (capturing strengths and areas for improvement)	Low	Medium	Useful	Medium
3 Hybrid processes (e.g. capturing data by a mix of interviews, questionnaires, focus groups etc.)	Medium	Good	Useful	High
4 Questionnaires or checklists.	Low	Poor	Non existent	Medium

1 Using an award-style 75-page report for self assessment
1.1 Producing the report

Organizations producing written internal 'applications' typically form a multi-functional team to go out and gather the data, write the document and edit it into its final format. Assigning ownership of particular criteria from the model is often a key element in compiling and writing the report. For although team members may be asked to gather data on a number of elements of the model, the most effective approach to the management of both this, and the writing phase, is to nominate an overall criterion or category owner for each part of the model.

Experience has shown that team members need not only report-writing skills, but must also be trained to understand the framework being used, and how the assessment process operates. Such training helps the report writers to get inside the mind of the assessors so that they understand how to present their organization in a way that will lead to a fair reflection of the organizations current position.

1.2 Scoring the 'report'

The next important stage in the process is the establishment of an assessor team. Some organizations rely on the experience of businesses like the Bristol Quality Centre to assess an internal 'application', others also see benefits in training their own internal assessors. A combination of the two is common and can help to deepen understanding and to increase the sense of ownership of the self assessment exercise, whilst maintaining the credibility of the overall assessment and scores achieved.

It is normal practice for teams of four to six internal assessors to be trained using the same training materials and 'calibrated' case studies as those used to establish the EFQM pool of award assessors. In this way, companies can ensure an internal consistency in the assessment process.

It is common that internal assessments use the same team approach as that applied to the actual award applications. It is important and beneficial to note that despite the common training that team members will have been given in understanding the model and developing assessment skills, there will still be variations in judgement applied from one assessor to another. This variation will be caused in part by what they do or do not absorb from the application, their past experiences in business, their own perceptions of excellence and how critical they are likely to be of evidence presented. So, although a consistency in approach to assessment can be achieved, such variations cannot be eradicated, and neither should they be. Like the witnesses at the scene of a crime, assessors each have their own perceptions which, when examined collectively, can present a highly accurate overall picture of events. It is, therefore, important that assessment is not undertaken by just one individual.

Ideally, what is needed is a balanced team, and it is up to each organization to decide what this comprises in their case. However, as a general rule it will include members from different functions, with different background experience and levels of optimism. And above all, it will offer as rounded a view of corporate excellence as possible. The assessment team should not just consist of 'quality' specialists!

As part of the assessment, it may be appropriate to undertake the equivalent of an award 'site visit'. This can be used to clarify and verify some of the issues raised by the application. But this must be approached with caution. A site visit can be misunderstood as a means of questioning the integrity of the original application writers and is thus not very helpful in establishing ownership of any improvement actions resulting from the assessment. However, if the assessors are drawn from other divisions of the organization, it may be necessary for them to undertake a site visit in order to gain a better understanding of the unit being assessed. In such an instance, members of the original writer team can be jointly involved with the assessors in this process of increasing understanding. In this way, friction is avoided, and a sense of ownership of the findings is increased.

As a compromise between 'no site visit' and a 'full site visit', some organizations arrange for the 'assessors' to meet with the 'writers' to explore areas of the application that caused debate and uncertainity as to the true achievement of the organization.

1.3 Feedback report

Whether a site visit is undertaken or not in either case the crucial part of the self assessment process is the feedback report. This clearly identifies the strengths and areas for improvement of the organization, and indicates a measure of its progress towards corporate excellence through the scoring profile achieved.

This report, unlike many others that the management team may have received, provides a balanced picture rather than just a catalogue of bad news. The assessment also has a measurement result which clearly positions the organization with respect to both the model and the other excellent organization using it. If the report is written in the positive tone recommended by the award processes, then it should be received as a vital instrument to redirect an improvement strategy or to increase the momentum of its implementation.

The feedback report in the award process highlights the applicant's position without stepping over the line of attempting to provide solutions or telling the management team how to run their organization. It is a great advantage if an internal feedback report can offer the same degree of neutrality as would be expected of an external assessor team. If this style or report can be produced sucessfully, it is more likely to be accepted as a fair judgement of the organization against the chosen framework.

1.4 Advantages and disadvantages of 'award style process'

Basing your internal assessment on the award process creates the advantage of knowing that you are using a well tried and tested yardstick. The fact that it is being used by many others allows you to make some direct comparisons with the results of others through self assessment networks (see Appendix 2). The detailed nature of the data gathering process ensures sufficient depth to give an accurate judgement of the organization. This adherence to accuracy is further enhanced by training those involved to the same level as that of the award assessors.

The disadvantages found in using the full application report approach relate mainly to the lack of ownership of the process by senior managers. If they have not been involved in the data gathering process, they may question the validity of the information being used. If they have not been involved in the assessment, they may question the credibility of the conclusions and score. Assessors need a detailed level of understanding of the framework and assessment process, which requires time-consuming training and assessment plus the time required for the preparation of feedback often means that it is difficult to involve senior managers directly.

2 Using a facilitator-led workshop approach

2.1 The workshop approach

A different approach to self assessment, which sets out to address the issue of ownership, is the perception-based workshop. Chapter 6 provides an outline for this approach. This approach is based around the executive team of an organization or business coming together in a workshop environment to undertake a 'live' assessment of their business against an agreed framework. The proformas in Chapter 6 provide a basis for preparing for such a workshop.

As a minimum, each member of the team should be briefed about the award framework, and given an outline of the nature of the process to be undertaken. They can then gather their thoughts about how they see their organization in relation to each of the award criteria before coming to the event.

During the workshop, the team will compile lists of strengths and areas for improvement against each of the elements of the framework. With appropriate facilitation, they can be prompted to ensure that they have addressed all the relevant areas. This facilitation also needs to provide some external calibration (and possibly also moderation!) to arrive at a consensus score for each item or criterion within the model. Indeed, the whole model can be addressed in one workshop, and there is an advantage in the team seeing their entire organization against the model in one exercise. However, if more time is needed to discuss the issues, the model can be addressed in sections over a series of meetings.

The above process is based solely on the perceptions of that team. The most senior management team may not have the same view as those closer to the coal face and so, to arrive at a wider consensus, it may be appropriate for the team undertaking the assessment to gather some data before the event. This data-gathering process may involve assimilating existing results and canvassing views on the deployment of various approaches at different levels in the organization. To ensure the effectiveness of this data-gathering activity it is normal to provide some training for those involved.

In deciding what resources to apply to this process, it is important for the senior management team to establish what they intend to do with the results gleaned from the workshop. The better the quality of input data, the more credible the output in determining priorities and action plans. However, the law of diminishing returns applies, and if intensive data-gathering is felt to be necessary, then perhaps the production of a 75-page document is more appropriate.

2.2 Advantages and disadvantages of the workshop approach

The main advantage of the workshop process is that it requires less time to conduct than other self assessment activities - and this makes it easier to involve senior management. When the senior management team have undertaken the assessment themselves, not only is there a greater understanding of the relevance of the framework to their organization, but there is also a much greater feeling of involvement in the results of the process. The greater involvement means that there is more follow-through from the assessment into the development of action plans, and provision of resources.

A disadvantage of this process, can be that the level of accuracy of the assessment appears to have been compromised. This can be the result of a perceived inadequacy in resources applied to data-gathering, and the lack of training given to those carrying out the assessment. It may also be difficult to undertake direct comparisons either externally or with other business units. Our experience in large organizations which use both approaches outlined above suggests that workshop assessments tend to score higher than 75-page 'application' assessments.

3 Hybrid tailoring of a review method to suit your business
3.1 The hybrid approach
The first decision facing companies considering tailoring a method of review relates to the need to strike a balance between creating a model specific to the needs of their particular organization, and having a process that facilitates external comparisons.

For most companies it is essential that the framework of criteria used is aligned to one of the two main award processes. This provides a common language for sharing best practice. In some instances elements have been added to the standard model, although this has happened more frequently in respect of the Malcolm Baldrige National Quality Award than among those using the European Quality Award. However, in most cases, the only tailoring undertaken has involved taking the existing framework elements and 'translating' the language into the jargon of the organization, linking it to specific internal initiatives which management can identify.

A second decision relates to the choice of an appropriate focus before or during site visits, for different methods of data collection. One typical solution is for a team of assessors, who are normally from other business units, to plan a site visit lasting around a week, during which they gather sufficient data to assess, i.e. they use the site visit, itself, to make the assessment with little or no pre-analysis being done by the unit being assessed.

In order to manage expectations and elicit early participation from the local unit management team, many of these reviews are preceded by a brief workshop assessment event. This not only raises the level of understanding of the management team, but begins to involve them closely in planning the review.

Additionally, in advance, the team may distribute a questionnaire addressing key areas of the framework. Completed questionnaires can be summarized to focus activities during the site visit week.

The site visit is likely to take the form of a series of discussions with individuals or groups of people ranging from one-to-one structured interviews, to focused discussion groups led by members of the assessor team.

Data is thus accumulated and mapped out against the framework to present an overall picture of the business unit's current position. The picture is a blend of existing performance measures, the detailed perceptions of a good slice of the organization's people and evidence of deployment of key approaches.

The culmination of all this activity is the judgement by the assessor team of the unit's performance, measured against the corporate excellence framework. First, each individual assessor determines the strengths, areas for improvement and score, then a team consensus is sought by bringing together these combined judgements. The results of the team consensus are then translated into a feedback report, similar to that produced in the award process, and that is then presented to the management team of the business unit. This type of corporate excellence review is summarized in the figure below which outlines the approach adopted by the UK's Royal Mail and now replicated by several organizations.

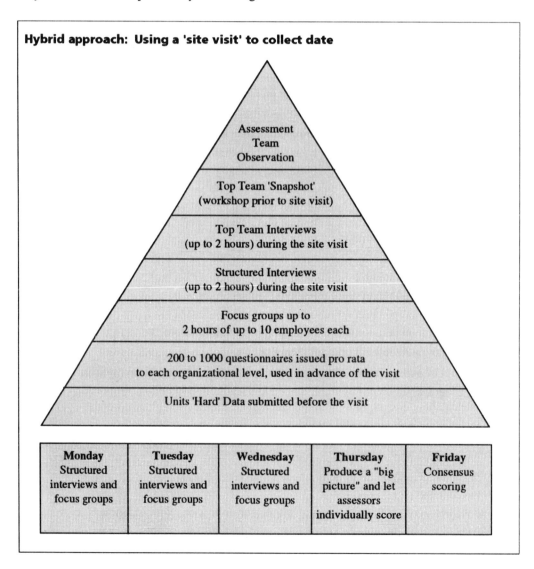

Hybrid approach: Using a 'site visit' to collect date

Assessment Team Observation

Top Team 'Snapshot' (workshop prior to site visit)

Top Team Interviews (up to 2 hours) during the site visit

Structured Interviews (up to 2 hours) during the site visit

Focus groups up to 2 hours of up to 10 employees each

200 to 1000 questionnaires issued pro rata to each organizational level, used in advance of the visit

Units 'Hard' Data submitted before the visit

| **Monday** Structured interviews and focus groups | **Tuesday** Structured interviews and focus groups | **Wednesday** Structured interviews and focus groups | **Thursday** Produce a "big picture" and let assessors individually score | **Friday** Consensus scoring |

3.2 Advantages and disadvantages of hybrid approaches

To make such a process effective, it is typically believed to be important that the assessor team is chosen from the ranks of senior personnel who, in the main, have experience in operational line management. Some functional specialists may add strength to the team, but the main characteristic of the process is that of a peer group review.

With such a team, it is more likely that the results will be accepted and that the management's effort is then focused on reviewing and implementing their improvement strategy. It is worth reiterating at this point the importance of a team approach in making a judgement through this type of review process. In our experience, these reviews cannot be successfully undertaken by an individual, in particular a quality specialist, with a checklist approach to auditing the organization.

There are many difficulties in 'taking out' a group of senior managers to perform such an intensive review process. The most significant is the time taken up by training, planning the review, the actual site visit and the follow-up to present results. In order to minimize the impact on senior managers' schedules, and to make effective use of such a high level resource, it is important to provide support in the form of coordination and logistics. Therein lies a potential role of the quality specialists in the organization.

There are many benefits to be gained from involving senior managers in such peer group reviews. In larger organizations there is often a need to break down barriers that are erected when areas of the business focus too much on their own internal results, rather than on the processes necessary to achieve them. The involvement of senior managers combats this by establishing a forum for sharing best practice from one division to another. This sharing of best practice is done at a level where decisions can be taken to implement change when clear benefits have been demonstrated.

4 Questionnaires or check-lists ... relative strengths

Although there are questionnaires that attempt to analyze the European Quality Award in all its nine criteria, these are designed primarily to generate awareness about the process. More detailed questionnaires are often used to focus on the need for data in areas such as customer satisfaction, employee satisfaction and leadership. These are typically used within one of the previously described processes.

It should be noted that any questionnaire approach will typically deliver only a number, band or grade 'answer'. The essential identification of strengths and/or areas for improvement that are necessary for use in improvement planning, can not be obtained from this approach.

Summary

Although there is a wide consensus on the frameworks, there is no universal blueprint for implementing a self assessment process. It is necessary for each organization to develop its own strategy. Many organizations 'mature' from perhaps an initial 'workshop' approach to the collection of more detailed information through hybrid or written processes.

Appendix 2

Bibliography, References and Suggested Reading

The list below contains a mixture of reference materials with additional suggested reading. They are listed in order of appearance, or relevance by chapters.

Chapter 2

1. Kano, N (1993) 'The Right Way to Quality', EOQ '93, Proceedings. pp 125-131. Helsinki, Finland.
2. Kano, N (1989) 'Quality Sweating Theory; Crisis Consciousness Vision and Leadership', Hinshitsu, Volume 19, Number 4, pp 32-42 (In Japanese).
3. Camp, Robert C 'Benchmarking; The Search for Industry Best Practices that Lead to Superior Performance' (1989). ASQC Quality Press.
4. EFQM Viewpoint, the TQM magazine December 1993. MCB University Press.

Chapter 4

5. National Institutes of Standards and Technology (USA), (1994). 'Malcolm Baldrige Award Criteria'. American Society for Quality Control.
6. Self Assessment based on the European Model for Total Quality (1994). The European Foundation for Quality Management, Brussels.
7. Zemke, Ron, and Schaaf, Dick (1989). 'The Service Edge; 101 Companies that Profit from Customer Care' New York; New American Library.
8. The Forum Corporation. (1988). Customer Focus Research - Executive Briefing. Boston.
9. Technical Assistance Research Programmes Institute. (1986). Consumer Complaint Handling in America; An Update Study, Washington DC.
10. AT & T. (1990). Achieving Customer Satisfaction; AT & T Quality Technology Centre, Technical Publications.
11. Demming, W E (1986). Out of the Crisis. MIT Centre for Advanced Engineering Studies, Cambridge, MA.
12. Covey, Stephen R (1992). Principal Centered Leadership. Simon & Schuster.
13. Harrington, James H (1987). The Improvement Process. McGraw-Hill.
14. Drucker, Peter F Managing for the Future (1992). Butterworths-Heinemann Ltd.
15. Popplewell, B and Wildsmith, A (1989). Becoming the Best. Gower, London.

Organizations that may be helpful

American Society for Quality Control (ASQC)
ASQC assists in administering the USA's Malcolm Baldrige National Quality Award program under contract to NIST (see overleaf). ASQC is dedicated to facilitating continuous improvement and increased customer satisfaction by identifying, communicating and promoting the use of quality principles, concepts and technologies. ASQC strives to be recognized throughout the world as the leading authority on, and champion for, quality.

Contact Address:
> **American Society for Quality Control**
> **P O Box 3005**
> **Milwaukee**
> **WI 53210 - 3005**
> **USA**
> **Tel: +1 414 272 8575**
> **Fax: +1 414 272 1734**

Bristol Quality Centre (BQC)
Bristol Quality Centre is one the UK's centres of excellence for support with quality and business improvement. Established in 1982 it has developed a most impressive track record of successful change in the public, manufacturing and service sectors.

From a base within the University of the West of England, Bristol Quality Centre offers:

- A Self Assessment Network (see "Business Excellence Self Assessment Network" overleaf)
- Training processes to assist self assessment and to create assessment teams
- Scoring workshops
- Consultancy to assist self assessment and/or award applications
- EFQM licenced training programmes

Contact Address:
> **Bristol Quality Centre**
> **P O Box 54**
> **Fishponds**
> **Bristol**
> **BS16 1XG**
> **United Kingdom**
> **Tel: +44 (0) 272 763932**
> **Fax: +44 (0) 272 585116**

British Quality Foundation (BQF)

The overall objectives of the BQF are to:

- Promote wider understanding of total quality and assist every type of UK organization in its implementation.
- Identify and publicize outstanding role model organizations practising TQM through the operation of a prestigious UK quality award scheme.
- Act as the UK's authoritative voice on issues of quality, both domestically and internationally.
- Play a pivotal role in the future development of quality management in the UK by giving coherence to, and creating consensus among, those groups interested in quality.

Overall direction is provided by the Board of Directors. The five founding directors are: Sir Denys Henderson, Chairman of ICI, (President and Chairman of the Board), Peter Bonfield of ICL, Michael Hepher of British Telecom, Michael Heron of The Post Office, and Ken Sanders of Texas Instruments.

Contact Address:

The British Quality Foundation
Vigilant House
120 Wilton Road
London
SW1V 1JZ
United Kingdom
Tel: +44 (0) 71 931 0607
Fax: +44 (0) 71 233 7034

Business Excellence Self Assessment Network (BESAN)

The Business Excellence Self Assessment Network is a network of organizations whose purpose is to provide a practical forum for sharing best practice on the implementation of business excellence self assessment processes.

The Business Excellence Self Assessment Network provides:

- Quarterly structured meetings at member sites
- Access to database listing members and their areas of interest in self assessment
- Quarterly newsletters updating on award processes and members' successes
- Confidential scoring profile database available to members
- Detailed exchanges of information relating to specific improvement initiatives
- Member task teams reporting on relevant issues

Details from:

Business Excellence Self Assessment Network

P O Box 54

Fishponds

Bristol

BS16 1XG

United Kingdom

Tel: +44 (0) 272 763932

Fax: +44 (0) 272 585116

European Foundation for Quality Management (EFQM)

The EFQM was founded by the Presidents of 14 major Western European organizations in September 1988. Its objectives, mission and vision is as follows:

Objective

The EFQM believes that, through Total Quality management, Western Europe will become a leading force in the world market. EFQM's objective is to create conditions to enhance the position of European industry by strengthening the role of management in quality strategies.

Mission

EFQM's mission is to:

- Support the management of Western European companies in accelerating the process of making quality a decisive influence for achieving global competitive advantage
- Stimulate and, where necessary, assist all segments of the Western European community to participate in quality improvement activities and to enhance the quality culture.

Vision

EFQM's vision is to become the leading organization for promoting and facilitating Total Quality Management in Western Europe. This vision will be achieved when TQM has become an integrated value of the European society, and European management has achieved a global competitive advantage.

The European Quality Award, launched in 1991, is a key focus of the organization.

Contact address:

European Foundation for Quality Management

Avenue des Pléiades 19c

B-1200 Brussels

Belgium

Tel: +32 2 775 3511

Fax: +32 2 779 1237

United States National Institute of Standards and Technology (NIST)

Responsibility for the Malcolm Baldrige National Quality Award (MBNQA) is assigned to the US Department of Commerce. NIST, an agency of the Department's Technology Administration, manages the Award Programme.

NIST's goals are to aid US industry through research and services; to contribute to public health, safety and the environment; and to support the US scientific and engineering research communities. Much of NIST's work relates directly to quality and to quality-related requirement in technology development and technology utilization.

Working closely with NIST there is "The Foundation for the Malcolm Baldrige National Quality Award".

The Foundation was created to foster the success of the Programme. The Foundation's main objective is to raise funds to permanently endow the Award Programme.

Prominent leaders from US companies serve as Foundation Trustees to ensure that the Foundation's objectives are accomplished. Donor organizations vary in size and type and are representative of many kinds of organizations and business groups. To date, the Foundation has raised approximately $11 million.

Contact address:

Malcolm Baldrige National Quality Award
National Institute of Standards & Technology
Route 270 and Quince Orchard Road
Administration Building Room A537
Gaithersburg
MD 20899-0001
USA
Tel: +1 301 975 2036
Fax: +1 301 948 3716

Appendix 3

How to score against the European Quality Award framework
1. Why is scoring important?

For most people involved in assessing their organization, the main aim of the exercise is the identification of a list of strengths and, perhaps more importantly, areas for improvement. The belief is that by doing this, and then using the information to compose action plans, assessors will be able to drive the organization forward. So why is scoring important?

Our experience has shown that management teams can easily agree about strengths and areas for improvement in the own part of its organization. However, if they are then asked to give a score to reflect their perception of the organization's achievement as a whole against those strengths and areas for improvement, responses reveal wide variations.

This means that, even though there has been agreement on the issues, there are significant differences of opinion about either their relative importance or the persvasiveness of the strengths or areas for improvement. In such circumstances, there can clearly be no satisfactory agreement about the way forward or, indeed, how much effort is required to effect improvement.

Thus, the purpose of scoring is not just to give an organization an overall mark for performance, but also to enable the management team to compare their assessment with that of their colleagues and then to come to a consensus which positions the organization's current level of achievement as they together see it.

2. Background to scoring methods

So, to enhance the credibility of the application of corporate excellence models, it is necessary to ensure that scoring is consistent. This is vital in generating confidence and in determining whether or not an organization has moved forward.

The problem is that the scoring of corporate excellence models is not an exact science and does require a heavy element of judgement. It is not the simple application of a checklist with 'yes' or 'no' answers. Even so, it is still possible to achieve considerable consistency in scoring as long as the scorer has been fully trained in the use of the scoring mechanism.

When scoring an organization, trained assessors are expected to be able to conform to a band of around plus or minus 70 points out of a total potential score of 1,000 points. And although, as has been previously stated, this book is not intended to provide the means for readers to become fully trained assessors, it is necessary to be generally familiar with the scoring process in order to glean a fuller knowledge of these models of corporate excellence, and the criteria on which they are based.

In understanding the elements of scoring, the first factor to be established is that for both 'enabler criteria' and 'results criteria' the scoring structure is two dimensional. For instance, when scoring 'enablers', assessors are looking at the performance in two dimensions, namely the 'efficacy of the approach' and the 'degree of the deployment' that has been achieved in implementing the approach throughout the organization.

Similarly, when looking at 'results' one is looking both at the 'excellence of the actual results' achieved, and at the 'scope, or breadth of coverage of the results' presented.

Enablers Analysis (Keywords)		Results Analysis (Keywords)	
Approach	Deployment	Results	Scope
Soundly based	Little usage	Positive trends	Relevant
Systematic	Half	Comparisons	Few
Prevention	Full potential	- own targets - external	Some
Integration		Results caused by approach	Many
Review			Most
Refinement		Best in class	All
Role model		Leadership maintained	

Looking first to the factors used when determining a score for an 'enablers', the table above lists the elements that one would be looking for in determining the degree of excellence of the approaches used within the organization. Most of the terms used in the table are self-evident, but one or two would benefit from further clarification; for example what is meant by 'review'. In this context the assessor is not just seeking to ensure that the approach is actually applied within the organization - this is known as compliance checking and is more in the domain of ISO 9000 considerations. Rather, we are looking for a review to ascertain or confirm that the original purpose of the approach is actually being achieved in a business effective manner. We want to know if improvements designed to achieve a better approach have been determined, and if those improvements in the approaches have been, and are being, implemented.

Similarly, the aspect of 'integration' can cause some mystification. In examining this, we are looking to ensure that the approach that has been put forward to satisfy this requirement of the criteria, is now contributing as an essential component of the organization rather than as a 'bolt-on' extra. We have found that the best way of explaining what is meant by 'good integration' of an approach or process is to ask people to consider whether, if that approach or process were discontinued tomorrow, the organization would notice its passing. If the organization would carry on just as before, one would suspect that 'good integration' had not been achieved.

The other dimension to be considered when scoring an enabler is that of deployment which, on the face of it, seems a simple concept. It would appear that all one has to do is elicit an estimation of the actual breadth and depth of the application of an approach, and then assess the degree to which it has been applied - compared with its full potential - throughout the organization. However, in practice it is relatively rare for there to be a common and shared understanding of the degree of deployment. So, while the table on the previous page lists the requirements of deployment, the practice of determining a score can lead to a lively debate!

Similarly for the results criteria the table lists the requirements that would be considered when determining a score, i.e. for both the 'results' and the 'scope of the results' dimensions.

With the help of additional information contained within the 'scoring charts' (overleaf), assessors are able to score each of the two dimensions of an enabler or results criteria.

3. Using the EFQM scorecards

Charts 1 and 2 on the first tear out page provide the scoring metrics that EFQM assessors use. Chart 1 should be applied for Enabler Criteria and Sub-criteria (1-5) and Chart 2 for Result Criteria (6-9)

A percentage score should be assigned for each criteria/sub-criteria. The second tear out page provides a scoring summary to record individual percentages and to convert overall or average percentages to weighted award 'points'.

The analysis of strengths and areas for improvement, for each criteria/sub-criteria should be completed before using the scoring cards (see chapter 6.3). For guidance, we would offer the following two observations. The first is that the requirements that must be met to achieve a particular score should not be seen as consisting of a set of absolute hurdles, meaning that each and every requirement has to be achieved in order for that percentage score to be given. Rather, the requirements cited, say, for a 50% score (see charts), should be seen as a series of guidelines; so it is possible for an organization to score a 50% or perhaps slightly higher score even though it has not absolutely achieved an adequate performance in all aspects relevant to that percentage scoring point. It is, therefore, possible for an organization to offset the good or over-achievement in, say, three of the requirements with an under-achievement in one of them.

Another point of guidance is that more consistent scoring appears possible if the assessor starts by **assuming** the achievement of the organization is that compared with the requirements meriting a 50% scoring. Then, if that is not suitable as a score, a move either towards zero or towards 100% is made, depending on whether the organization is worse than, or better than, the requirements in the guidelines for a 50% score.

The advice given to assessors when they are considering an organization's performance against a criteria is to score each of the two dimensions separately, so they will ultimately have two scores for each of the elements that together contribute to an enablers or a results performance (e.g. Approach and deployment, for an enabler).

But how do you combine the scores of the two dimensions? The normal approach is to start by taking the arithmetic average of the two percentage scores given for each of the two dimensions. However, this can lead to some disturbing results particularly when there are significant differences between the scores for the two dimensions. This is even more the case when one of the scores for a dimension is close to zero.

The approach has therefore been refined over the years to the effect that the arithmetic average is viewed as the starting point for conclusions. Once this average has been determined, the assessor should then consider whether this properly reflects the organization's performance on a linear scale from zero, i.e. 'this organization has achieved nothing' - to a 100% score, ie 'this organization is as good as one could reasonably expect in today's situation'. 50% is not an 'average' score. Award winning organizations' total scores are typically only 750 points, or less, out of the 1000 possible.

Final note: only quartile percentage scores or 10% increments have been used in all the examples presented. Indeed, the general observation is that one should stick either to quartiles or to 10 % increments when scoring, even when giving an average for the two dimensions. The system is no more accurate than that, particularly for the novice scorer.

4. Using 'snapshot' scorecards
Readers using this process for the first time may be prepared to sacrifice a small degree of scoring 'purity' and accuracy in exchange for a simpler and potentially easier to apply scoring system. The snapshot scorecards on the third tear out page, coupled with the scoring summary on the fourth tear out page provide such a method.

Readers should first complete the analysis of strengths and areas for improvement for each criteria/sub-criteria (see chapter 6.3) and then make the 'scoring decisions' illustrated on the third tear out page.

EFQM Scorecard

Chart 1 The Enablers

The Assessor scores each part of the Enablers criteria on the basis of the combination of two factors.

1. The degree of excellence of your approach
2. The degree of deployment of your approach

Approach	Score	Deployment
Anecdotal or non-value adding.	0%	Little effective usage.
Some evidence of soundly based approaches and prevention based systems. Subject to occasional review. Some areas of integration into normal operation.	25%	Applied to about one-quarter of the potential when considering all relevant areas and activities.
Evidence of soundly based systematic approaches and prevention based systems. Subject to regular review with respect to business effectiveness. Integration into normal operations and planning well established.	50%	Applied to about half the potential when considering all relevant areas and activities.
Clear evidence of soundly based systematic approaches and prevention based systems. Clear evidence of refinement and improved business effectiveness through review cycles. Good integration of approach into normal operations and planning.	75%	Applied to about three quarters of the potential when considering all relevant areas and activities.
Clear evidence of soundly based systematic approaches and prevention based systems. Clear evidence of refinement and improved business effectiveness through review cycles. Approach has become totally integrated into normal working patterns. Could be used as a role model for other organizations.	100%	Applied to full potential in all relevant areas and activities.

For both 'Approach' and 'Deployment', the Assessor may choose one of the five levels 0%, 25%, 50%, 75%, or 100% as presented in the chart, or interpolate between these values.

EFQM Scorecard

Chart 2 The Results

The Assessor scores each part of the Enablers criteria on the basis of the combination of two factors.

1. The degree of excellence of your results
2. The scope of your results

Results	Score	Scope
Anecdotal.	0%	Results address few relevant areas and activities.
Some results show positive trends. Some favourable comparisons with own targets.	25%	Result address some relevant areas and activities.
Many results show positive trends over at least 3 years. Favourable comparisons with own targets in many areas. Some comparisons with external organizations. Some results are caused by approach.	50%	Results address many relevant areas and activities.
Most results show strongly positive trends over at least 3 years. Favourable comparisons with own targets in most areas. Favourable comparisons with external organizations in many areas. Many results are caused by approach.	75%	Results address most relevant areas and activities.
Strongly positive trends in all areas over at least 5 years. Excellent comparisons with own targets and external organizations in most areas. "Best in Class" in many areas of activity. Results are clearly caused by approach. Positive indication that leading position will be maintained.	100%	Results address all relevant areas and facets of the organization.

For both 'Results' and 'Scope', the Assessor may choose one of five levels 0%, 25%, 50%, 75%, or 100% as presented in the chart, or interpolate between these values.

Points Scoring Summary using EFQM Score Cards

	Approach %	Deployment %	Overall %	Total Points Awarded (Weighted)
1 Leadership 1a 1b 1c 1d 1e 1f Average %				Average % x 1.0 =
2 Policy and Strategy 2a 2b 2c 2d 2e Average %				Average % x 0.8 =
3 People Management 3a 3b 3c 3d 3e Average %				Average % x 0.9 =
4 Resources 4a 4b 4c 4d Average %				Average % x 0.9 =
5 Processes 5a 5b 5c 5d 5e Average %				Average % x 1.4 =
	Result %	Scope %	Overall %	
6 Customer Satisfaction				Overall % x 2.0 =
7 People Satisfaction				Overall % x 0.9 =
8 Impact on Society				Overall % x 0.6 =
9 Business				Overall % x 1.5 =
				Total Points =

'Snapshot' Scorecard: Chart 1. Enablers

Decision 1. Score Approaches				
Doing Nothing	Just Starting	Some relevant approaches in place	Many proven relevant well integrated approaches	Role model approaches fully integrated into normal working practices
Score 0	1	3	5	7

Note: A relevant approach should be systematic and prevention based

Decision 2. Score Deployment				
Not Started	Less than 25% of full potential	Less than 50% of full potential	Less than 75% of full potential	Deployed to full potential
Score 0	2	6	10	14

Note: The deployment assessment is a summary of the breadth and depth of the application of all relevant approaches to all relevant parts of the unit

Decision 3. Score Evaluation Processes			
Occasional or non-existent	Some evidence of review and refinement	Regular reviews and evidence of change/improvement	All approaches regularly reviewed and improvements implemented
Score 1	3	5	7

Note: review refers to systematic, regular checks of the business effectiveness and the subsequent improvement of the relevant approach(es)

Criteria	Decision 1 Score	Decision 2 Score	Decision 3 Score	Total Score (1+2+3)	X Factor	Predicted %
1a					3.125	
1b					3.125	
1c					3.125	
1d					3.125	
1e					3.125	
1f					3.125	
2a					3.125	
2b					3.125	
2c					3.125	
2d					3.125	
2e					3.125	
3a					3.125	
3b					3.125	
3c					3.125	
3d					3.125	
3e					3.125	
4a					3.125	
4b					3.125	
4c					3.125	
4d					3.125	
5a					3.125	
5b					3.125	
5c					3.125	
5d					3.125	
5e					3.125	

Transfer % scores to Points Scoring Summary Overleaf

'Snapshot' Scorecard: Chart 2. The Results

Decision 1. Scope of Measurement

Few or no relevant measurements	Some to many measurements of relevant parameters	Regular measurement of most relevant direct and indirect parameters	Regular measurement of all relevant direct and indirect parameters
Score 1	3	5	7

Note: Relevant means proven to be of value to the appropriate stakeholder(s)

Decision 2. Trends and Levels of Results

On balance, negative trends exist	Some positive trends and satisfaction comparison with own targets	Positive trends over 3+ years and many favourable comparisons with own targets	Strongly positive trends over 3+ years and favourable comparisons with own targets in most areas	Strongly positive trends in all relevant results for 5+ years. Excellent comparisons against own targets
Score 0	2	6	10	14

Note: Trends should be demonstratable by readily available data sources

Decision 3. 'Benchmarking' of Results

No external comparison	Some external comparisons made	Favourable comparisons with external organizations in relevant areas	Excellent Comparisons with competitors and/or best in class organizations
Score 1	3	5	7

Note: 'benchmarking' in this context refers to the comparison of levels and trends with competitors and/or best in class organizations

Criteria	Decision 1 Score	Decision 2 Score	Decision 3 Score	Total Score (1+2+3)	X Factor	Predicted %
6					3.125	
7					3.125	
8					3.125	
9					3.125	

Transfer % scores to Points Scoring Summary Overleaf

Points Scoring Summary using Snapshot Score Cards

	Predicted Overall %	Total Points Awarded (Weighted)
1 Leadership 1a 1b 1c 1d 1e 1f Average %		Average % x 1.0 =
2 Policy and Strategy 2a 2b 2c 2d 2e Average %		Average % x 0.8 =
3 People Management 3a 3b 3c 3d 3e Average %		Average % x 0.9 =
4 Resources 4a 4b 4c 4d Average %		Average % x 0.9 =
5 Processes 5a 5b 5c 5d 5e Average %		Average % x 1.4 =

	Result %	Scope %	Overall %	
6 Customer Satisfaction				Overall % x 2.0 =
7 People Satisfaction				Overall % x 0.9 =
8 Impact on Society				Overall % x 0.6 =
9 Business				Overall % x 1.5 =
				Total Points =

☐ Please supply details of the European Quality Award

☐ Please supply details of the benefits of membership of the European Foundation for Quality Management

Name ....

Address...

....

....Post Code...................................

Tel No: ....Date ....

☐ Please supply details of the UK Quality Award

☐ Please supply details of the benefits of membership of the British Quality Foundation

Name ....

Address...

....

....Post Code...................................

Tel No: ....Date ....

☐ Please supply details of Chapman & Hall's bulk purchase rates

☐ Please provide details of Chapman & Hall's customization service (200+ copies)

☐ Please register my name for updates as they become available

☐ Please supply details of the Business Excellence Self Assessment Network

Name ....

Address...

....

....Post Code...................................

Tel No: ....Date ....

European Foundation for Quality Management
Avenue des Pleiades 19c
B-1200 BRUSSELS
Belgium

The British Quality Foundation
Vigilant House
120 Wilton Road
LONDON
SW1V 1JZ
UK

Bristol Quality Centre
PO Box 54
Fishponds
Bristol
BS16 1XG
UK